Standard Grade | Foundation | General

English

Leckie × Leckie

First exam published in 2000.
Published by Leckie & Leckie, 8 Whitehill Terrace, St. Andrews, Scotland KY16 8RN tel: 01334 475656 fax: 01334 477392
enquiries@leckieandleckie.co.uk www.leckieandleckie.co.uk

ISBN 1-84372-297-6

A CIP Catalogue record for this book is available from the British Library.

Printed in Scotland by Scotprint.

Leckie & Leckie is a division of Granada Learning Limited, part of ITV plc.

Acknowledgements

Leckie & Leckie is grateful to the copyright holders, as credited at the back of the book, for permission to use their material. Every effort has been made to trace the copyright holders and to obtain their permission for the use of copyright material. Leckie & Leckie will gladly receive information enabling them to rectify any error or omission in subsequent editions.

[BLANK PAGE]

F

0860/401

NATIONAL QUALIFICATIONS 2000

TUESDAY, 16 MAY
10.35 AM – 11.25 AM

ENGLISH
STANDARD GRADE
Foundation Level
Reading
Text

Read carefully the passage overleaf. It will help if you read it twice. When you have done so, answer the questions. Use the spaces provided in the Question/Answer booklet.

SCOTTISH QUALIFICATIONS AUTHORITY

MCB 0860/401 6/32020

Adapted from an article by Audrey Ronning Topping.

Charlie, Our M

With a gleam in his eye and mischief in mind, he had us all under his spell.

1 I first met Charlie on Cat Street in Hong Kong. I was browsing for antiques when I heard a terrible screech and turned to see a beggar squatting on the kerb beside a balding, scruffy, white cockatoo.

2 Chained to a wooden perch, the bird was surrounded by children who were teasing him with sticks. The children laughed when the half-crazed creature snapped back at them with his hooked beak, flared his yellow crest and shrieked in Chinese. I was overcome with admiration. This little creature was a fighter.

3 I wanted to rescue him but could not bear the thought of keeping a bird in a cage. As I started to walk away, the cockatoo looked at me imploringly and said, "OK, OK, OK."

4 I was hooked. How did he know I spoke English? After some haggling, I bought him.

5 At home, I removed his shackle. He was grateful and, doglike, began following me round the flat. He couldn't fly because the beggar had cut his flight feathers, so he waddled like a duck and used his beak and claws to hoist himself up our potted trees.

6 In the wild, baby cockatoos learn survival from their parents and other members of the flock. Now, in captivity, Charlie began imitating the only flock he knew, my family.

7 Charlie had a remarkably quick mind and good memory and was soon calling us by name.

8 Every day he picked up new words. His first phrase was "Hello Charlie" and then "Hello" to anyone within range, then "Shut the door!" which soon became "Robin, go back and shut the door."

9 His most frequent word was "Why?" Often when I spoke to the children, Charlie would ask "Why?" just as they did. It drove me crazy. I finally shouted back, "Because I'm your mother!" That became his next phrase.

10 Before long we could see the results of our love and care. Charlie's feathers grew thick and glossy. He developed a confident glint in his eye and established himself as top of the pecking order with our four cats who, to my amazement, restrained their killer instincts even when Charlie stole their food.

11 We were convinced he would never fly again. But one day, after months of watching the children play in the courtyard below the flat, he suddenly dived off the balcony, glided eight storeys down on his crippled wings and made a three-point landing—claws and beak—on the shoulder of Susan.

12 The surprised children shouted, "Super Charlie!" and swung him round in circles on the end of a long stick. He loved it. Soon he called out "Super Charlie" each time he landed in the courtyard.

13 When we moved to Scarsdale, New York State, Charlie became an instant celebrity, greeting everyone with "Hello there! How ya doing?"

14 He slept in the kitchen, where he acted as watchbird, but spent most of his time in an old apple tree in the garden. There he hacked out a large apartment for himself with two entrances and several peepholes. Charlie could not fly up or take off without help, but in the mornings he would hoist himself up with his beak and claws, and glide from tree to tree. In the evening he would call "Audrey!" or "Robin!" until one of us came to bring him inside.

15 Charlie spoke English to us and Spanish to our housekeeper. He meowed to the cats and barked and whistled to our three dogs. They came obediently when he called, and guarded him from stray animals in the garden.

16 Unlike the other members of our family, he was a good listener. We were convinced he could understand everything we said. He could keep a secret, too, so we spilled out all our problems to him. I encouraged this because he was cheaper than a psychiatrist. Eventually we began to think of Charlie as a person of importance.

17 Before I knew it, 25 years had passed.

ad, Bad Cockatoo

18 One clear blue Sunday afternoon we prepared a barbecue in the garden for Joanna's birthday. Charlie was perched on the top branch of a tall tree, with about 20 fat crows he hung out with. They had become friends over the years—Charlie spoke fluent crow and allowed them to share his apples.

19 Surrounded by his crows, Charlie was in his element. Every few minutes he would hang upside down by one leg, flap his wings and shout, "Super Charlie!"

20 Suddenly the calm was shattered by his screams. We looked up to see two large hawks diving out of the sky, straight for Charlie. One hawk grabbed him in its talons and began to fly away.

21 The crows took off after the invading hawks like fighter planes attacking a bomber, cawing to signal other crows to join them. They soon formed a thick black cloud above the hawks and prevented them from gaining height.

22 The evil birdnappers flew out of the garden and headed across a busy street. Joanna and I ran below, shouting and flailing with sticks while the crows flew above, circling and dive-bombing. Motorists screeched to a halt.

23 Finally the crows forced the hawk into a tree. We watched in astonishment as Charlie escaped while his winged allies held the enemy at bay.

24 For one glorious minute, he really was Super Charlie. In his heroic battle, he at last flew high—like the free spirit he was meant to be.

25 Then the second hawk rocketed down, snatching him from above. We heard one last scream. Dear Charlie. He died a champion.

26 That evening, the birthday celebration became a funeral as the whole family gathered to pay respects to one of our own. We saved a few yellow crest feathers and buried him in the garden.

27 Charlie was composed of the stuff that legends are made of, and in our family he has become just that. None of us will ever forget the adventures we shared for 25 years with Charlie Cockatoo.

[*END OF PASSAGE*]

[BLANK PAGE]

FOR OFFICIAL USE

F

Total Mark

0860/402

NATIONAL QUALIFICATIONS 2000

TUESDAY, 16 MAY
10.35 AM – 11.25 AM

ENGLISH STANDARD GRADE

Foundation Level
Reading
Questions

Fill in these boxes and read what is printed below.

Full name of centre

Town

Forename(s)

Surname

Date of birth
Day Month Year

Scottish candidate number

Number of seat

NB Before leaving the examination room you must give this booklet to the invigilator. If you do not, you may lose all the marks for this paper.

SCOTTISH QUALIFICATIONS AUTHORITY
©

DO NOT WRITE IN THIS MARGIN

QUESTIONS

Write your answers in the spaces provided.

Look at Paragraphs 1 and 2.

1. What first drew the writer's attention to Charlie?

____________________ 2 0

2. **Write down two** things which show that Charlie was not well looked after by the beggar.

(i) ____________________ 2 1

(ii) ____________________ 0

3. "This little creature was a fighter." (Paragraph 2)

(*a*) **Write down three separate words** the writer uses to describe how Charlie reacted when the children teased him.

2 1 0

(*b*) How did this behaviour make the writer feel about Charlie?

____________________ 2 1 0

Look at Paragraphs 3 and 4.

4. (*a*) Why did the writer not rescue Charlie immediately?

____

____________________ 2 0

(*b*) What **two** things persuaded her to rescue him?

(i) ____________________ 2 1

(ii) ____________________ 0

DO NOT WRITE IN THIS MARGIN

5. **Write down** the expression which tells us that the writer did not pay as much as the beggar asked for Charlie. 2 0

Look at Paragraph 5.

6. Explain fully why Charlie began following the writer "doglike" round the flat. 2 1 0

7. Explain fully why Charlie had to use his beak and claws to "hoist himself up our potted trees". 2 1 0

Look at Paragraphs 6 to 9.

8. **Write down** the word which the writer uses to compare her family to Charlie's family in the wild. 2 0

9. What did Charlie do which showed he had "a remarkably quick mind and good memory"? (Paragraph 7) 2 1 0

[Turn over

DO NOT WRITE IN THIS MARGIN

Look at Paragraphs 10 to 12.

10. How did Charlie's **appearance** and **behaviour** change as a result of the family's love and care?

2 1 0

11. Explain clearly what was amazing about the cats' attitude to Charlie.

2 1 0

12. Explain fully why the children were "surprised". (Paragraph 12)

2 1 0

Look at Paragraphs 13 and 14.

13. Despite becoming an "instant celebrity" (Paragraph 13), what things does Charlie do which remind us he is a bird?

2 1 0

Look at Paragraphs 15 and 16.

14. Explain why the family "began to think of Charlie as a person of importance".

2 1 0

DO NOT WRITE IN THIS MARGIN

Look at Paragraph 17.

15. Why do you think the writer has made this sentence a short paragraph on its own?

____ 2 0

Look at Paragraphs 18 and 19.

16. Explain fully how Charlie and the crows had become friends.

____

____ 2 1 0

17. " . . . Charlie was in his element."

Explain how the rest of Paragraph 19 helps you to understand the meaning of this expression.

____

____ 2 1 0

Look at Paragraphs 20 to 23.

18. (*a*) **Write down three** expressions the writer uses to make the attack seem warlike.

(i) ____

(ii) ____

(iii) ____ 2 1 0

(*b*) Choose any **one** of these expressions and **explain how well** you think it helps to describe what happened.

____

____ 2 0

[Turn over

DO NOT WRITE IN THIS MARGIN

19. "Motorists screeched to a halt." (Paragraph 22)
What **two** things caused this?

(i) ______________________________

(ii) ______________________________ 2 1 0

Look at Paragraphs 24 to 27.

20. **Write down** the word which shows how fast the second hawk moved.

2 0

21. "For one glorious minute, he really was Super Charlie." (Paragraph 24)
Which expression in this paragraph explains why the writer thought this?

______________________________ 2 0

Think about the passage as a whole.

22. Read the following statements and then tick (✓) to show whether each is TRUE, FALSE or CANNOT TELL from the passage.

	TRUE	FALSE	CANNOT TELL	
The Toppings lived in Hong Kong for 25 years.				2 0
The Topping family had three dogs and four cats.				2 0
Charlie died on a Saturday afternoon.				2 0

23. "None of us will ever forget the adventures we shared for 25 years with Charlie Cockatoo." (Paragraph 27)
Which adventure do you think is most memorable and why?

____

____

______________________________ 2 1 0

[*END OF QUESTION PAPER*]

[BLANK PAGE]

G

0860/403

NATIONAL QUALIFICATIONS 2001

MONDAY, 14 MAY
1.00 PM – 1.50 PM

ENGLISH
STANDARD GRADE
General Level
Reading
Text

Read carefully the passage overleaf. It will help if you read it twice. When you have done so, answer the questions. Use the spaces provided in the Question/Answer booklet.

MCB 0860/403 6/71520

The Appeal of

1 All the junk in Scotland meets your befuddled gaze: thousands of unwanted gifts, the "wee something" for Christmas and the "I saw this and thought of you" for your birthday (how you wish they hadn't); then there are the holiday souvenirs. In short, all the stuff with which we tend to clutter our lives and our cupboards has somehow ended up in one place, awkwardly arranged on a vast number of folding tables.

2 Behind them, all kinds of people are perched on the tailgates of a variety of vehicles. Is this some bizarre store for recycled rubbish? Well, in a way it is. In other words, you have found yourself in the middle of your first car boot sale. They can be found most weekends in summer, and sometimes in winter too, in villages, towns and cities throughout the country. Sometimes they are held on an occasional basis—a charity or other organisation will hire a hall or a school playground, advertise in the local press and rent out pitches at £5 or £10 for the day. Other sales are held every Saturday or Sunday on more permanent sites.

3 Women seem to outnumber men behind the essential tables: although men often come to help to set up, they retire shyly for most of the day and return in the late afternoon to pack up the left-overs. Curiously enough, there are as many male customers as female: all human life wanders by.

4 There goes a plump medallion man who will tell you—his unhappily captive audience—a succession of unfunny and wildly politically incorrect jokes at which you will laugh, lamely, and hope he goes away.

5 There goes a succession of polite elderly gentlemen, clean and smart in their car coats; they will go off happily clutching boxes of your ancient gardening tools to which their wives will most surely object, but who are you to spoil their fun?

6 There is, just occasionally, a serious side to all this, which may affect the buyer rather than the genuine seller. Car boot sales can provide a certain amount of cover for less honest traders and it is as well to bear this in mind if you are offered a more than average bargain. Where, for instance, did those big canisters of cleaning fluid designated "Janitorial Supplies" originate? And what about those suspiciously home-made looking video cassettes of all the latest movies? Trading Standards Officers sometimes visit boot sales to keep a lookout for fakes. Police

Never underestimate what will sell. Old console games or market for all

occasionally find stolen goods lurking among the junk. Customs and Excise may be investigating those suspiciously cheap cigarettes and Environmental Health Officers may even be wondering whether that delicious home-made tablet has been concocted with due regard to public health.

7 But on the whole, say the police, they have little trouble with car boot sales. Most are legitimate and harmless: ordinary punters offloading bric-a-brac onto other ordinary punters. To a Martian hovering up there we must all look like nothing so much as a colony of ants, struggling to carry off various large and cumbersome objects, a table here, a suitcase there . . .

8 So if you fancy trying a boot sale, just for the fun of it, here are a few ground rules for participating in this most rewarding game.

9 Go as a buyer first, if you can. Have a good look around. Some pitches are better than others. Some are closer to the loos. Some are on windy corners and some may be right next to the little roundabout that plays the same four-bar tune all day long.

10 Go early, if you are selling. Many car boot sales that advertise an opening time of 10 am are being set up by seven or eight in the morning.

Car Boot Sales

videos will disappear as if by magic and there is a ready
kinds of gadgets.

11 Beware of the antique dealers. They will surround your table at this early hour like wild dogs around a carcase, fingering your Aunty Annie's floral teapot with its dripping spout and trying to decide if they are getting the bargain of the century at £1·50 including chipped lid. Remember the Antiques Roadshow. Remember that daft little pottery owl that fetched thousands.

12 Invest in a cheap wallpapering table. You can sell out of the boot of your car, but if you have as much junk to get rid of as most of us do, you will need more space than the average hatchback can supply. Take a secure container for your money—preferably a money belt so that you can keep your takings safely about your person. Don't leave handbags lying around; car boot sales are hunting grounds for purse snatchers. By the same token it's wise to take a friend. Then you have someone to mind the stall while you take time out to browse around the neighbouring stalls.

13 Don't sell old electrical goods: they can be dangerous, and you can be in trouble with the law for doing so.

14 Take lots of food and drink with you: sandwiches, chocolate bars, flasks of tea and coffee, cans of soft drinks. You will be amazed at how hungry and thirsty you will get standing around all day and there is little point in blowing your takings on hamburgers although the smell will certainly drive you wild. Wear comfortable shoes and remember to take warm clothes, even in summer. Remember to plan for rain. This is Scotland after all, and you will probably get cold and wet.

15 Don't overprice your goods, but never underestimate what will sell either. The truth is that people will buy almost anything if the price is right. Old Playstation games, or genuine second-hand videos, will disappear as if by magic. Even more surprisingly, so will large, rickety (and empty) wooden boxes, elderly baseball caps that were given free with something ten years ago, shabby plastic dinosaurs that have been in many an imaginary battle and a pile of kitchen gadgets such as the tattie peeling machine that always took ages to wash afterwards, the expensive plastic containers with ill-fitting lids and the pancake mixer that liberally sprinkled you with batter every time you tried to use it. Just lay it out and somebody will come along wanting to buy it.

16 Above all, don't expect to make any fortunes. What you will do is recycle a truly astonishing amount of junk, give an amazing amount of pleasure to all kinds of people, observe all human life wandering past your table, and come home with a modest profit. That's if you can stop yourself from filling your car boot with other people's junk before you go home.

17 After all there's a little collection of pressed glass over there that is so irresistible, and the old hand-knitted Shetland shawl that nobody seems to have spotted, and isn't that a genuine stone hot-water bottle lurking among the rubbish . . . ?

Adapted from an article in "The Scotsman" by Catherine Czerkawska.

[*END OF PASSAGE*]

[BLANK PAGE]

FOR OFFICIAL USE

G

Total Mark

0860/404

NATIONAL QUALIFICATIONS 2001

MONDAY, 14 MAY
1.00 PM – 1.50 PM

ENGLISH
STANDARD GRADE
General Level
Reading
Questions

Fill in these boxes and read what is printed below.

Full name of centre

Town

Forename(s)

Surname

Date of birth
Day Month Year

Scottish candidate number

Number of seat

NB Before leaving the examination room you must give this booklet to the invigilator. If you do not, you may lose all the marks for this paper.

SCOTTISH QUALIFICATIONS AUTHORITY

DO NOT WRITE IN THIS MARGIN

QUESTIONS

Write your answers in the spaces provided.

Look at Paragraphs 1 and 2.

1. "All the junk in Scotland meets your befuddled gaze"

   How does the writer continue the idea of "junk" in the first two paragraphs?

   As he goes on to explain ~~that~~ all the worthless presents that people recieve

   2 1 0

2. **Write down an expression** from Paragraph 2 which shows that the writer thinks this "junk" makes a **strange collection**.

   "some Bizzare store for recycled rubbish"

   2 1 0

3. Explain the **differences** between the two types of car boot sale described in Paragraph 2.

   (i) Some carboot sales are helded occational for charity

   2 1 0

   (ii) Some are on a weekly basis held on ~~with~~ more permanent sites

   2 1 0

Look at Paragraphs 3 to 5.

4. (*a*) When it comes to selling, women "seem to outnumber men".

   Write down the expression the writer uses to suggest why the men don't do the selling.

   Men often come to help set up but they retirer shyly for most of the ~~afternoon~~ day

   2 0

   (*b*) When it comes to buying, there are "as many male customers as female".

   What is the writer's reaction to this? Answer in your own words.

   His reaction is that their are a wide variety of people who go to Carboot Sales.

   (all human life wanders by)

   2 0

DO NOT WRITE IN THIS MARGIN

5. (*a*) The writer gives two examples of "human life" wandering by.

In your own words, explain as fully as you can why the writer:

(i) disapproves of the "plump medallion man" ____________________

____ 2 1 0

(ii) might sympathise with the "succession of polite elderly gentlemen".

____ 2 1 0

(*b*) Explain fully what the writer gains by using the expression "There goes . . ." to introduce these two examples.

____ 2 1 0

Look at Paragraphs 6 and 7.

6. Explain **in your own words** what the writer means by the "serious side" of car boot sales.

____ 2 1 0

7. (*a*) What do each of the following organisations look for at car boot sales?

(i) Trading Standards ____________________

(ii) Police ____________________ 2 1 0

(iii) Customs and Excise ____________________

(*b*) Explain what concerns the Environmental Health Officers might have about any food on sale.

____ 2 1 0

DO NOT WRITE IN THIS MARGIN

8. **Write down** an expression which shows that there are very few concerns about the "serious side" of car boot sales.

Most carbootsales are legitimate & harmless

2 0

Look at Paragraphs 8 to 14.

9. In Paragraph 8 the writer introduces the idea of giving practical advice.

How does the sentence construction at the beginning of Paragraphs 9 to 14 help to show this?

By getting right to the point in the first sentence of every paragraph.

2 0

10. (*a*) **Write down** the simile or comparison which describes how the antique dealers behave.

They will surround your table at this early in the morning like wild dogs around a carcase.

2 0

(*b*) Explain what is appropriate about this comparison.

As the dogg would grabb the carcase & eat it the antique dealers will grab your things & buy them.

2 1 0

11. From Paragraph 12, **explain in your own words** why:

(*a*) you should "invest in a cheap wallpapering table".

So you can just take it down and sell it out of the back of your car.

2 1 0

(*b*) you would be "wise to take a friend".

So you can have some one to look after the stall while you have a look at the other sales.

2 1 0

DO NOT WRITE IN THIS MARGIN

Look at Paragraph 15.

12. "... people will buy almost anything ..."

The writer gives several examples to prove this statement.

Choose any **two** (APART FROM GAMES AND VIDEOS).

In each case explain why the writer thinks it is surprising that anyone should buy them.

(i) wooden Boxes, the writer makes it clear that he is surprised that people buy them as he says they are rickety and empty. making the reader think they are worthless. 2 1 0

(ii) plastic dinosaurs, the writer makes it clear again that it is worthless by saying that it is shabby. 2 1 0

Look at Paragraphs 16 and 17.

13. The writer believes several benefits can be gained from car boot sales. **In your own words** describe two of them.

(i) give enjoyment to other people from your junk. 2 1 0

(ii) getting out and meeting new people.

14. What do you think the writer is suggesting by her descriptions of the items in Paragraph 17? 2 1 0

The writer is making ~~them~~ the items seem so tempting to buy, but has said before that you cant be sure that you will come home with other peoples junk.

15. Why does the writer use ellipsis (...) at the end of the final sentence? 2 0

Think about the passage as a whole.

16. Look at the photograph which accompanies the article.

Explain how it shows examples of the following:

(i) the writer's advice being taken The buyers are observing the items closely before they buy.

(ii) the writer's advice being ignored The seller is only himself, he didn't take a friend, so he cant leave the stall to have a look around. 2 1 0

[Turn over for Question 17 on *Page six*

DO NOT WRITE IN THIS MARGIN

17. Tick (✓) **one** of the following expressions which you think **best** describes the writer's purpose in this article.

Explain your choice by detailed reference to the text.

to provide information ✓   to entertain ☐

to be thought-provoking ☐

I chose that as I believe that the story contains mostly information to the reader about what to do in car boot sales.

2
1
0

[*END OF QUESTION PAPER*]

[BLANK PAGE]

F

0860/401

NATIONAL QUALIFICATIONS 2002

TUESDAY, 7 MAY
10.35 AM – 11.25 AM

ENGLISH
STANDARD GRADE
Foundation Level
Reading
Text

Read carefully the passage overleaf. It will help if you read it twice. When you have done so, answer the questions. Use the spaces provided in the Question/Answer booklet.

SCOTTISH QUALIFICATIONS AUTHORITY

The House

Who needs a hutch? It's time to bring your rabbit in from the cold. *Gillian Ferguson* investigates the fastest-breeding trend in indoor pets.

ABOVE: a young fan with Jack and Smokey,

1 Cats – pah, old hat. Dogs – ha, they've had their day. Roll over Rover and pack that catnip, Cuddles – cats and dogs are yesterday's pets. There's a hot new furry friend on the block – the house rabbit. Forget hutches and gardens, foxes and fields, today's rabbit is all about having a place in your home as well as your heart.

2 "The time for bunnies has definitely come," says Carolina James, director of the Rabbit Charity. "They are the pet of the future. A big revolution is coming, and within a generation we predict the house rabbit will be the most popular pet in the UK."

3 The growing number of bunny-lovers are finding out there's a lot more to rabbits than carrots and breeding like, er . . . friendly, playful, loving, and – importantly, when a rabbit is living in your burrow – easily house-trained. They can also learn to come when called, recognise words, respond to commands and open doors.

4 "In fact, they're smarter than some people," says rabbit-mad Ms James. "They can be as responsive as a dog, offering love and companionship, and are very charming and entertaining. They make excellent all-round family members." And if you work, the house rabbit is an ideal pet, being active in the morning before you go out, and the evening, just when you return – though a pair is better if you're out all day.

5 The first liberation of bunnies from their hutches was in America in the late 1980s, and the US House Rabbit Association has since been spreading the word. The bunny rush has now begun not just in the UK, but around the world, including the Far East, Canada and the Netherlands. The British House Rabbit Association was formed in 1996 with four members but now has some 3,000. "In the past year, it's just gone crazy, there's so much interest," says the Rabbit Charity's Scottish co-ordinator Fiona McBean. "People are realising that rabbits are not boring and have lots of character and affection, given the chance to express themselves." There are now local "Hopper Groups" for members to meet, a newsletter – called the *MacRabbit Runner* in Scotland, an annual Rabbit Convention, a national helpline dealing with everything from feeding problems to owners in distress, and 50 national advisers. "People can think we're very strange having a rabbit in the house," says Anne Mitchell, the Rabbit Charity's national administrator and treasurer. "But we're growing!"

6 And keeping rabbits in the house offers a far more natural life than the traditional hutch in the garden. In fact, locking up a rabbit is downright cruel. "Many, many rabbits are neglected or abused because people just don't realise they're doing horrible things," says Carolina James. People simply don't know that rabbits need companionship, exercise and toys. "They ignorantly keep them lonely and

Bunny Bug

two pet rabbits belonging to his aunt.

depressed, imprisoned in small hutches – the neighbours would call the RSPCA instantly if you kept a dog or cat like that."

7 Fiona McBean agrees: "People wouldn't dream of getting a puppy or kitten then stuffing it in a box at the bottom of the garden where it's only visited once or twice a day for a couple of minutes." This ignorance about how to care for rabbits was what prompted Carolina James to set up the Rabbit Charity several years ago, and launch International Rabbit Day to help get the message across.

8 "Bunnies Deserve Better" is the theme, and you can take part in fund-raising events, such as a "bunny sleep-in", where you sleep next to a bunny's bed in a sleeping bag; or you can phone the suitably named Bunny Hopline for advice and information; and there's "Something for Everybunny" at Bunny Buys, the charity's non-profit-making mail order and on-line shop. International Rabbit Day also saw the launch of the Carrot Top Awards to find "the world's top bunnies".

9 You could also sponsor a rescued bunny – a National Rabbit Aid survey found that there were at least 25,000 unwanted bunnies in animal shelters. Or actually adopt one – both organisations can link you to an SSPCA shelter in your area, and both recommend rescued rabbits. You can teach an older bunny new tricks and any rabbit can be house-trained, even one that has previously been outside. You also avoid rabbit adolescence when apparently sweetikins can temporarily turn into the "bunny from hell".

10 House training and bonding between bunnies and owners happen very quickly, with affectionate rabbits even licking their owners just as dogs do. Unlike dogs, however, rabbits don't need to be walked. Many enjoy following their owner around like a puppy and will invent ways to get your attention. "Soon they will have you wrapped round their little paws!" says Carolina James.

11 "You don't need television ever again," says rabbit fan John Smith, who has had indoor bunnies for the last two years. "Every evening they have a mad half hour where they hop and leap right into the air and toss their toys around – it's brilliant, really funny. My rabbit isn't just a pet, she's a friend – all the more so as I live alone." And the way he was rabbiting on it sounded like, with a house rabbit in his life, he was quite content.

Adapted from an article in *The Scotsman*.

[*END OF PASSAGE*]

[BLANK PAGE]

FOR OFFICIAL USE

F

Total Mark

0860/402

NATIONAL QUALIFICATIONS 2002

TUESDAY, 7 MAY
10.35 AM – 11.25 AM

ENGLISH
STANDARD GRADE
Foundation Level
Reading
Questions

Fill in these boxes and read what is printed below.

Full name of centre

Town

Forename(s)

Surname

Date of birth
Day Month Year

Scottish candidate number

Number of seat

NB Before leaving the examination room you must give this booklet to the invigilator. If you do not, you may lose all the marks for this paper.

SCOTTISH QUALIFICATIONS AUTHORITY

MCB 0860/402 6/31470

Marks

QUESTIONS

Write your answers in the spaces provided.

Look at Paragraphs 1 and 2.

1. " – cats and dogs are yesterday's pets." (Paragraph 1)

Write down two other expressions from Paragraph 1 which show they are no longer fashionable pets. **2 1**

(i) Cats – ______________________

(ii) Dogs – ______________________

2. **Write down** an expression from Paragraph 1 which shows that the house rabbit is the latest trend in pets.

______________________ **2 ■**

3. In what ways does the writer emphasise that we should think of today's rabbit as an **indoor** pet?

____

______________________ **2 1**

4. The expression "**f**urry **f**riend" is an example of a technique the writer uses in Paragraph 1.

Write down another example of this technique.

____

______________________ **2 ■**

PAGE TOTAL

Marks

Look at Paragraphs 3 and 4.

5. ". . . there's a lot more to rabbits than carrots and breeding like, er . . ." (Paragraph 3)

(*a*) How can you tell that the writer is hesitating here?

____

____ **2 1 0**

(*b*) Why do you think she hesitates?

____

____ **2 1 0**

(*c*) What does the writer think is the important feature of rabbits as indoor pets?

____

____ **2 1 0**

6. The writer uses the word "burrow" (Paragraph 3) instead of house or home.

Why is this a particularly suitable word to use here?

____

____ **2 1 0**

7. (*a*) **Write down two** qualities in rabbits which Ms James believes make them "excellent all-round family members". (Paragraph 4) **2 1 0**

(i) ____

(ii) ____

(*b*) Why does Ms James think the house rabbit is an "ideal pet" if you work during the day?

____

____ **2 1 0**

[Turn over

PAGE TOTAL

Marks

Look at Paragraph 5.

8. **Write down** the expression the writer uses to show that rabbits in America were kept like prisoners until the late 1980s.

______________________________ 2 ■ 0

9. ". . . the US House Rabbit Association has since been spreading the word."

Write down two pieces of evidence from Paragraph 5 which show that this has been successful in the UK. 2 1 0

(i) ______________________________

(ii) ______________________________

10. According to Fiona McBean, why is there "so much interest" in having rabbits as indoor pets?

____

______________________________ 2 1 0

11. How does the writer's punctuation help to show how enthusiastic Anne Mitchell is about the growth in rabbit ownership?

______________________________ 2 ■ 0

Look at Paragraphs 6 and 7.

12. (*a*) What **three** things do rabbits need that they don't get in the "traditional hutch in the garden" (Paragraph 6)? 2 1 0

(i) ______________________________

(ii) ______________________________

(iii) ______________________________

(*b*) How do the rabbits feel when they are kept "imprisoned in small hutches" (Paragraph 6)?

______________________________ 2 1 0

PAGE TOTAL

Marks

13. (*a*) How do **both** Carolina James (in Paragraph 6) **and** Fiona McBean (in Paragraph 7) emphasise the horrible treatment of rabbits?

____ **2 1 0**

(*b*) What **two** things did Carolina James do as a result of people's "ignorance about how to care for rabbits" (Paragraph 7)? **2 1 0**

(i) ____

(ii) ____

Look at Paragraphs 8 to 11.

14. Write down three of the fund-raising events of International Rabbit Day. **2 1 0**

(i) ____

(ii) ____

(iii) ____

15. Give **two** reasons why both rabbit organisations recommend "rescued rabbits" for adoption (Paragraph 9).

(i) ____

____ **2 1 0**

(ii) ____

____ **2 1 0**

[Turn over for Questions 16 to 19 on *Page six*

PAGE TOTAL

Marks

16. Write down two ways in which bunnies behave like dogs as pets. **2 1 0**

(i) ____________________________________

(ii) ____________________________________

17. Why does John Smith feel that "You don't need television ever again" (Paragraph 11)?

____

____________________________________ **2 1 0**

Think about the passage as a whole.

18. Write down an example of the writer's use of humour in this article.

____

____________________________________ **2 ■ 0**

19. The writer uses several quotations from interviews in her article.

How do these interviews improve the article?

____

____

____________________________________ **2 ■ 0**

[*END OF QUESTION PAPER*]

PAGE TOTAL

[BLANK PAGE]

G

0860/403

NATIONAL QUALIFICATIONS 2002

TUESDAY, 7 MAY
1.00 PM – 1.50 PM

ENGLISH STANDARD GRADE
General Level
Reading
Text

Read carefully the passage overleaf. It will help if you read it twice. When you have done so, answer the questions. Use the spaces provided in the Question/Answer booklet.

SCOTTISH QUALIFICATIONS AUTHORITY

1 The kettle switched itself off the boil with a sharp click. The young man filled the teapot with the steaming water and dropped in a teabag to add to the one already there. He sat the full pot on the formica-topped breakfast bar and made a silly face at his five-year-old daughter who was perched on a stool slowly getting through a bowl of milky porridge. Hearing his wife coming down the stairs from the bathroom he began to refill her mug but instead of entering the bright warm kitchen she lingered in the hall. He could hear her pulling on her heavy coat. She came in saying she had no time, she'd be late for her lift, her heels clattering on the tiled floor. She kissed goodbye to daughter and husband then was off in a whirl of newly-applied perfume and the swish of her clothes and the front door slamming.

2 He sat down on his stool and poured himself another mug of tea. He asked the child how she was doing, was the porridge too hot? She told him gravely that it was OK and went on making a show of blowing on each hot spoonful as she had been shown.

3 He picked up the newspaper that was lying folded open at the Situations Vacant pages. One advert was targeted in a ring of red felt-tip pen. The introduction was in big bold italics: ***"This time last year I was made redundant. Now I own a £150,000 house, drive a BMW and holiday in Bali. If you . . ."*** He opened out the paper and refolded it to the front page to check the headlines. The date he knew already but there it was: exactly one year he had been out of work.

4 Father and daughter chatted brightly as they strolled hand in hand down Allison Street heading for school. She was a talkative child and he would egg her on in her prattle for his own amusement. It was now well into the rush hour: traffic gushed by or fretted at red lights and urgent pedestrians commanded the pavements and crossings. It was bitter cold. He looked down at the girl to reassure himself that she was warmly enough dressed, but there was no need; he was well used to getting her ready. Her round reddened face was the only prey to the cold air and she beamed up at him, quite content.

5 At the last corner before the school's street they both halted in an accustomed way and he squatted down to give her a kiss. She didn't mind the ritual but not outside the gates: her pals might see and that would be too embarrassing. He tugged her knitted hat a little further down her forehead and tucked in a couple of strands of her long reddish hair. They could hear the kids' voices laughing and shouting from the playground. They waved cheerio at the gate and he stood watching until she was inside and with her friends, then he turned away. He was vaguely aware of one or two mothers doing likewise and one or two car doors slamming. With both gloveless hands shoved into the pockets of his cream-coloured raincoat he made for home. Behind him the bell began to sound above and through the high excited voices.

* * * * *

6 He finished writing the letter and signed his name with a brisk underline, printing it in brackets below, just in case. Picking up the CV from the coffee table he glanced over the familiar details of his education and career. It looked good, he thought, organised, businesslike. His wife had managed to get a couple of dozen of them run off on her word processor at the office. It was the contents that struck him as pointless. What use was it to anyone to know what he had done at school? It was the grown man, someone with work experience, who was on offer, not the schoolboy. Not the kid who'd scuffed along, neither brilliant nor stupid, not the football-daft apprentice smoker who'd put his name to those long-forgotten exam papers then sauntered out carefree into the world. Well, maybe not carefree: he could still

remember some of the burdens and terrors of adolescence that he'd laugh at now. Then there was his five years of selling for the one firm. No problem there; those were good years. Their fruits were holidays abroad, marriage, the house, the baby. Plain sailing until the company had gone bust. Now he was no longer young and upwardly mobile. Not even horizontally mobile: stopped, stuck.

7 Referees. He always wanted to write the name of a football referee but didn't. What did people expect to hear from the names he always supplied—"Don't touch this character, he's a definite no-user"? It was just wee games, this form-filling. He believed it was the interview that would count, if only he could land one.

8 He arranged the letter and CV together, tapping sides and tails until there was no overlap, then folded them in half and in half again. The envelope was ready, briskly typed by his wife on the old manual machine she used for home typing jobs. As he made ready to lick the stamp he stopped suddenly. He'd done it again, folding the sheets in half twice. That was clumsy, unprofessional-looking. The way she'd shown him was much better: folding one third then another so that you only had two folds instead of three. Gingerly, he tried to reopen the envelope but it was stuck fast and the flap ripped jaggedly. He'd have to type another one himself in his laborious two-fingered style. His first go had two mistakes and so he typed another one, slowly, making sure he got everything right.

* * * * *

9 He kept walking, on past the pillar-box at the corner of their street. That one was definitely unlucky: nothing he had ever posted there had brought good fortune. No, he would carry on to Victoria Road whose offices and air of industry made it feel a more hopeful point of departure. As he reached the main thoroughfare he saw a mail van pull up at the postbox he was heading for and he quickened his pace. He watched the grey-uniformed driver jump down and unlock the red door; he broke into a run. The pillar-box yielded a bulky flow of mail to the driver's hand combing it into his big shapeless bag. The young man handed over his letter with a half-smile although his heart had sunk. One letter in all that flow of paper. And how many were job applications piled randomly, meaninglessly on top of one another? His own would soon be lost in that anonymous crowd. It seemed to him now more than ever like buying a raffle ticket, like doing the football coupon every week. What chance had you got?

10 But it was easy standing here to recall the bustle of business life. It came to him how much he wanted it, that activity. It was more than just something you did to make money: it was the only life he knew and he was missing out on it, standing on the sidelines like a face in the crowd at a football game. If it wasn't for the child, he thought, he wouldn't have the will to keep on trying. He checked his watch: the kids would soon be coming out.

* * * * *

11 He waited at their corner, hands deep in pockets, his shoulder to the dirty grey sandstone wall. The bell was ringing and he could hear the children streaming out into the playground. When she spotted him she broke into a trot and he retreated round the corner a little to swoop suddenly with a mock roar, bearing her laughing wildly up into his arms. As he set her down he asked quite formally what kind of morning she'd had. She began to speak, and her enthusiasm breathed upwards into his smiling face and beyond in the chill air.

Adapted from the short story "Application" by Michael Munro

[*END OF PASSAGE*]

[BLANK PAGE]

FOR OFFICIAL USE

G

Total Mark

0860/404

NATIONAL QUALIFICATIONS 2002

TUESDAY, 7 MAY
1.00 PM – 1.50 PM

ENGLISH
STANDARD GRADE
General Level
Reading

Fill in these boxes and read what is printed below.

Full name of centre

Town

Forename(s)

Surname

Date of birth
Day Month Year

Scottish candidate number

Number of seat

NB Before leaving the examination room you must give this booklet to the invigilator. If you do not, you may lose all the marks for this paper.

SCOTTISH QUALIFICATIONS AUTHORITY

Marks

QUESTIONS

Write your answers in the spaces provided.

Look at Paragraphs 1 to 3.

1. Why did the young man have time to make breakfast for his wife and daughter?

As he was out of work. 2

2. From the last sentence in Paragraph 1, **write down two separate words** which suggest his wife was in a hurry.

Whirl	Swish

2 1

3. (*a*) In Paragraph 1, why is "**perched**" a particularly suitable word to describe how the five-year-old girl sat on her stool?

~~As she was hunched over her poridge which she didnt like & perched most describing what she had been like at the table~~

As the 5 year old was small so there for looked perched like a bird as the stool was high. 2 1

(*b*) Give **two** pieces of evidence to show that the daughter treated the business of eating her breakfast seriously.

(i) with every spoonful of poridge she brew on it, just like she was shown. 2 1

(ii) The word "gravely" is used ~~which~~ before she speaks to her dad which means that she was serious. 2 1

4. Why do you think one advert in the newspaper was "targeted in a ring of red felt-tip pen" (Paragraph 3)?

As he wanted the same as it said in that article a BMW, 150,000 to own and holidays. 2 1

PAGE TOTAL

Marks

Look at Paragraphs 4 and 5.

5. What did the young man enjoy about the walk to school with his daughter? **Answer in your own words.**

He enjoyed her talking and he would keep her talking all of the walk to school. (egg her on) encourage

2 1 0

6. The writer uses a colon (:) in Paragraph 4 (after "rush hour") and in Paragraph 5 (after "outside the gates").

Tick (✓) the box to show which you think is the correct reason for its use in each case.

2 1 0

	Paragraph 4	*Paragraph 5*
To introduce a quotation		
To elaborate on an idea	✓	
To introduce an explanation		✓

7. Write down **two** examples of **separate words** the writer has used to convey the idea of "rush hour".

trassic gushed	fretted at red lights

? 2 1 0

8. "It was bitter cold." (Paragraph 4)

Explain clearly how later in Paragraph 4 the writer makes the cold air seem alive.

It explains this by saying, "her round reddened face was the only prey to the cold air." which means where face was the only thing that was not covered.

2 1 0

[Turn over

PAGE TOTAL

Marks

9. (*a*) Why is the father's kiss described as a "ritual" (Paragraph 5)?

As it must happen every time that the father walks her to school.

2 1

(*b*) Which expression earlier in Paragraph 5 helps you to understand the meaning of "ritual"?

At the last corner before the school street the both haulted in an accustomed way.

2 ■

10. ". . . but not outside the gates . . ." (Paragraph 5)

Using your own words as far as possible, explain why the daughter made this condition.

As it tells the reader that ~~her~~ friends ~~would make~~ fun She would be embarresst.

2 1

Look at Paragraphs 6 and 7.

11. (*a*) What did the man think "looked good" about his CV?

That it was organised & buisnesslike.

2 ■

(*b*) What **two** things about "this form-filling" did he think were "pointless"?

In each case explain **why** he thought so.

(i) What the Person did at School – it didnt matter what happened at School it mattered about the man now.

2 1

(ii)

2 1

PAGE TOTAL

Marks

Look at Paragraph 8.

12. (*a*) Why did the man not put the stamp on the envelope? with a name on it

As he had sent the CV to the Same People and they didnt give him a interview

2 1 0

(*b*) "Gingerly, he tried to reopen . . . flap ripped jaggedly."

How does the structure of this sentence emphasise the man's care in reopening the envelope?

The sentence structure ~~describes~~ emphasises his carefulness not to rip the ~~letter~~ envelope

2 1 0

(*c*) **Write down** the **two** expressions the writer uses in this paragraph to show the contrast between the man's typing skills and his wife's.

2 1 0

(i) She had Briskly typed up

(ii) He'd have to type another on in his laborious two-fingered style.

Look at Paragraphs 9 and 10.

13. Explain clearly why the man chose to post his letter in Victoria Road.

As there was an air of hope on that street with its offices an industry it felt secure for him that he would hear good news.

2 1 0

14. Explain clearly why "his heart had sunk" (Paragraph 9) when he handed over his letter.

As he thought that his little letter felt ~~small~~ forthless in all that ~~many~~ letters.

2 1 0

[Turn over for Questions 15 to 17 on *Page six*

PAGE TOTAL

Marks

15. " . . . standing on the sidelines like a face in the crowd at a football game." (Paragraph 10)

Explain how effective you find this simile. 2 1 0

it is quite effective as it explain the let downs the man has had in the past with interveiws.

Think about the passage as a whole.

16. Throughout the passage, the man is shown to be thoughtful and caring about his daughter.

What evidence is there of this:

(*a*) in Paragraph 11? 2 1 0

(i) he found more strength in her enthusiasm.

(ii) He always was smiling when she was around.

(*b*) elsewhere in the passage? 2 1 0

(i) __________

(ii) __________

17. Overall, do you feel the story conveys a sense of **hope**, or of **despair**?

Tick (✓) the box to indicate your choice.

Hope	✓
Despair	

Justify your choice by detailed reference to the text. 2 1 0

I feel that the story portrays hope the man loves his daughter & wants to provide for her it is described at the end when it says her enthusiasm breathed on his face & in that same sentence it says he is smiling so it must have hope.

[*END OF QUESTION PAPER*]

PAGE TOTAL

32/58

[BLANK PAGE]

F

0860/401

NATIONAL QUALIFICATIONS 2003

TUESDAY, 6 MAY
10.35 AM – 11.25 AM

ENGLISH
STANDARD GRADE
Foundation Level
Reading
Text

Read carefully the passage overleaf. It will help if you read it twice. When you have done so, answer the questions. Use the spaces provided in the Question/Answer booklet.

SCOTTISH QUALIFICATIONS AUTHORITY

John, Me and the Lancashire Treasure

1 I learned the meaning of *gold fever* when I was thirteen — it came in the shape of thirty-three Roman coins dug out of the bed of a small stream on a West Lancashire farm.

2 A chance remark by a friend of my sister's that a hoard of coins had once been discovered about two miles from where I lived turned me, and my lifelong friend John Rimmer, into keen, young archaeologists. Our logic went: if 100 coins had been found there already then surely there must be a few more lying around undiscovered. There were, but getting at them was murder.

3 The trouble was that the Roman soldier, or whoever had originally owned them, had chosen the side of a stream in which to bury them. But unfortunately during the next nineteen hundred years or so the stream had slightly changed course until the coins were embedded in its bank or buried in the silt in the bottom.

4 When we first went coining it was the Easter holidays. Equipped with huge shovels and pans which we borrowed from the local farm we began the spine-bending task of shovelling silt from the bottom of the stream into a pan, carefully carrying the pan to a place where the water flowed more quickly, washing out the mud and then staring like fortune-tellers into tea leaves at the remaining collection of tiny pebbles for the dull coins we had been told about.

5 By mid-afternoon we were beginning to wonder whether some cruel joke had been played upon us and we took to catching tiddlers in our vacuum flasks, chasing the cows back from our site and hurling chunks of mud after a trespassing water rat. At tea-time, when our hearts were hardly in it, the boy from the local farm paid us a visit. It was he who had originally discovered the treasure.

6 "How many have you got?" he asked casually, leaning over the handlebars of his bicycle. "None," we answered dejectedly, half afraid even to look at him.

7 He grunted, climbed from his bicycle and clambered down the bank. "You're digging in the wrong place," he said. "You should be more over here." And taking my shovel from me he quickly filled the pan full of silt, washed it out and began to sift through the remains. Suddenly his hand shot forward like the tongue of a snake. "There you are," he said. "That's one!"

8 He passed me a dull piece of metal about the size of a five pence piece. It was a coin, but not much of a coin. "You have it," he said, "and dig in the right place next time." And with that he climbed back on his bike and pedalled away up the field. Putting the coin carefully into a purse we had brought for our anticipated treasure, we returned to our work with renewed enthusiasm. Before the day was out we had actually found a couple of our own, although none of them would have convinced a doubter. Nineteen hundred years had erased all their markings.

9 The next day we hit the jackpot. From virtually the first panning we pulled out three almost perfect coins, probably as clearly marked as when they had been originally buried. We had actually found treasure, proper treasure, with heads and names impressed upon it.

10 But suddenly the easy friendship which we had shared for years became stretched with tension as jealousy crept in.

11 We would peer together over the pan, each desperate to spot the next coin before the other. And now we began to make our own separate collections. We found the coins which had been overlooked, but, like a couple of gold-crazy prospectors, mutual distrust and envy had taken over.

12 For two weeks we worked that stream.

13 By now, of course, the whole river bank looked like something out of the Klondike, as heaps of rubble were tipped upon the grass after examination. We were less than pleased when the farmer's son came with the news that his father would like us to tidy up before we finished. By now we must have collected over twenty coins and we would pore over reference books in John's house trying to trace exactly what kind of coins we had found.

14 Then a strange thing happened: I lost one, and with it I lost interest. I know I had it on the bus going to school. But when I got there it had gone. John was livid. He was convinced I'd given it to the bus conductor by mistake.

15 All the fun of finding the coins was souring our friendship, so one day I just put all my share into a handkerchief, wrapped it up and gave it to my friend. "You'd better keep them," I said. "I don't trust myself not to lose the lot."

16 It was true, I didn't. And anyway, I had all kinds of new hobbies to be getting on with: there was chicken farming (all fifty died on me), mushroom growing, sword-collection (my mother eventually gave them to a house decorator) and rock and roll. The fun had been *finding* the coins. John was a much better bank than I was.

17 I went to see him a couple of years ago. He lives in New Zealand now and keeps them in a safe, all carefully labelled — apart from three very rare ones which apparently even puzzled the British Museum. And apparently people come from miles around to see his grand collection.

18 With great pride he carefully got them out for me and spread them across the dining table as we reminisced about who found which ones. At last, I asked nervously whether I might have one.

19 "One!" he said in astonishment. "You can take half of them. Choose any fifteen. They're yours. I've only been looking after them for you until you came to your senses."

20 I chose one. It was one I remembered finding. I still didn't trust myself with the rest. Apparently they're worth over £1,000 now and going up in value all the time.

21 It's a pretty wonderful thing to be thirteen years old and find buried treasure.

Adapted from an article by *Ray Connolly*

[*END OF PASSAGE*]

[BLANK PAGE]

FOR OFFICIAL USE

F

Total Mark

0860/402

NATIONAL QUALIFICATIONS 2003

TUESDAY, 6 MAY
10.35 AM – 11.25 AM

ENGLISH— STANDARD GRADE
Foundation Level Reading Questions

Fill in these boxes and read what is printed below.

Full name of centre

Town

Forename(s)

Surname

Date of birth
Day Month Year

Scottish candidate number

Number of seat

NB Before leaving the examination room you must give this booklet to the invigilator. If you do not, you may lose all the marks for this paper.

SCOTTISH QUALIFICATIONS AUTHORITY

Marks

QUESTIONS

Write your answers in the spaces provided.

Look at Paragraphs 1 and 2.

1. Where were the Roman coins discovered? 2 1 0

2. **Write down two** reasons why the writer and his friend became "keen, young archaeologists". 2 1 0

   (i)

   (ii)

3. **Write down an expression** which tells you that the coins were difficult to get to. 2 ■ 0

Look at Paragraph 3.

4. (*a*) Where had the original owner of the coins buried them? 2 ■ 0

   (*b*) Why had the coins moved from where they were first buried? 2 1 0

Look at Paragraph 4.

5. **Write down two pieces** of equipment the boys used to help them find the coins. 2 1 0

   (i)

   (ii)

PAGE TOTAL

Marks

6. **Write down an expression** which suggests that looking for the coins was hard work.

____ 2 ■ 0

7. Why do you think the writer uses the simile "staring like fortune-tellers into tea leaves"?

____

____ 2 1 0

Look at Paragraphs 5 and 6.

8. Why were the boys beginning to think by mid-afternoon that someone had played a cruel joke on them?

____ 2 ■ 0

9. Give **two reasons** why the visit of the local farm boy was important. 2 1 0

(i) ____

(ii) ____

10. **Write down the word** which describes how the boys were feeling about not finding coins.

____ 2 ■ 0

Look at Paragraphs 7 and 8.

11. What does the expression "his hand shot forward like the tongue of a snake" tell you about how the boy moved when he discovered the coin?

____ 2 1 0

12. **Write down two reasons** why the writer thought that it was "not much of a coin". 2 1 0

(i) ____

(ii) ____

[Turn over

PAGE TOTAL

Marks

13. **Write down an expression** which shows the effect that finding the coins had on the boys.

______________________________ **2 1 0**

Look at Paragraph 9.

14. Explain why the writer uses the expression "The next day we hit the jackpot".

____

______________________________ **2 1 0**

Look at Paragraphs 10, 11, 12 and 13.

15. (*a*) Which word **best** describes how the boys began to feel towards each other as they found more and more coins?

Tick (✓) the correct box.

Trusting	
Unselfish	
Suspicious	

(*b*) Give a reason for your answer.

____

______________________________ **2 1 0**

16. **Write down two things** which the boys did which show that they had become really interested in the coins. **2 1 0**

(i) ______________________________

(ii) ______________________________

PAGE TOTAL

Marks

Look at Paragraphs 14, 15 and 16.

17. What effect did the loss of the coin have on the writer?

____ **2 ■ 0**

18. How did John think the coin had been lost?

____

____ **2 1 0**

19. **Write down two reasons** why the writer gave his coins to his friend John. **2 1 0**

(i) ____

(ii) ____

20. Why is the word "*finding*" in italics?

____

____ **2 1 0**

Look at Paragraphs 17, 18, 19 and 20.

21. Where are the coins now kept?

____

____ **2 1 0**

22. Why were three of the coins not labelled?

____

____ **2 1 0**

[Turn over for Questions 23 and 24 on *Page six*

PAGE TOTAL

Marks

23. **Give two reasons** why, in your opinion, the writer chose only one coin. 2 1 0

(i) ______________________________

(ii) ______________________________

Think about the passage as a whole.

24. **Write down two things** that you have learned about "*gold fever*" from the passage. 2 1 0

(i) ______________________________

(ii) ______________________________

[*END OF QUESTION PAPER*]

PAGE TOTAL

[BLANK PAGE]

G

0860/403

NATIONAL QUALIFICATIONS 2003

TUESDAY, 6 MAY
1.00 PM – 1.50 PM

ENGLISH STANDARD GRADE

General Level
Reading
Text

Read carefully the passage overleaf. It will help if you read it twice. When you have done so, answer the questions. Use the spaces provided in the Question/Answer booklet.

SAB 0860/403 6/71570

We're out for the Count

Catriona Marchant and her children discover that Dracula has a big stake in Romania's tourist industry.

The door creaked open. A draught of cold air blew up from the stairs to the dark crypt and the hairs on our arms stood on end. The faint light from the flickering candle disappeared, there was a muffled scream, a sound of running footsteps and then some raised voices.

2 My three brave boys looked at each other and Douglas, the middle one, ran from the room. The eldest, Matthew, who had been taunting his younger brothers about being scared five minutes earlier, went a bit white and looked like he was going to change his mind about the visit.

3 We were in Dracula's castle — sited on the remote Tihuta mountain pass where the Victorian Gothic novelist Bram Stoker based the home of his fictitious vampire — two days' carriage ride from Bistrita in northern Transylvania.

4 Downstairs was Count Dracula's coffin in a narrow vault, the walls painted with the dramatic scenes of human victims, wolves, skulls, skeletons and the black-cloaked monster himself, red blood dripping from his pointed fangs. So far on our Romanian holiday the only blood-sucking had been from the mosquitoes in Bucharest. Luckily we had decided to send their father down first as a guinea pig to test out how scary this experience was likely to be for our seven-, five- and two-year-olds.

5 After the screams from the crypt, Matthew decided he would opt for a tour with the light on and I agreed. Even so there was a certain nervousness as we went down the stairs. Suddenly, Matthew let out a blood-curdling scream and jumped a foot in the air. "I've just seen a horrible blue hand with long nails, round the side of that door," he screeched.

6 One vampire hand was quite enough for a seven-year-old. Time for a drink and an ice-cream. As we walked up to the main lobby there was "Vampire" red wine for sale, glass vials of red liquid, wooden stakes and probably some garlic stashed under the counter.

7 As these tacky souvenirs revealed, it wasn't the real Dracula's castle but Hotel Castel Dracula, a three-star hotel built in the mountains to service some nearby ski slopes. The architecture (1980s mock castle) reflected the Dracula movies but the setting amid the dramatic scenery of the Tihuta pass is stunning. The "castle" is circled by bats every night and the surrounding forests have more wild bears and wolves than anywhere else in Europe.

8 Bram Stoker's story has become mixed up with the historical facts as the novelist based his blood-sucking fictional vampire on the 15th century bloodthirsty Prince Vlad Tepes. Vlad was known fondly as Vlad the Impaler.

9 The tourist board makes the most of this confusion between fiction and history, as the worldwide fascination with Dracula lures many a visitor to the country. The most well known sights are the birthplace of Vlad Tepes at the beautiful town of Sighisoara and Bran Castle, commonly known as Dracula's Castle.

10 Bran Castle is certainly dramatic, perched on the edge of a rock peak, its ramparts standing out against the dark mountain backdrop. But as it was the former summer royal residence, parts of it inside seem rather cosy and welcoming. The ruined castle of Rasnov seems a more suitable location for a Dracula film, with 360-degree views of the Carpathian Mountains after a steep walk up the wooded mountain.

11 Matthew did his best to scare the tourists. He had been reading his Dracula books and dressed up in a black cloak, cut out some paper fangs and jumped round corners and down steps.

12 He gained more smiles and laughs than any signs of horror — but then it was a warm, sunny August day. He completed his vampire outfit by choosing wooden daggers for himself and Douglas from the busy craft market to protect us from any blood-sucking monsters that might come our way (apart from mosquitoes).

Cloak and dagger: Alistair and Matthew had a scream fooling around near the birthplace of Vlad Tepes, the "original Dracula"

13 Dracula's Kiss was an extremely alcoholic, bright scarlet drink. This fiery concoction must have contained a large quantity of the local plum brandy, known as palinca. I drank this at the birthplace of Vlad Tepes in Sighisoara. His house is now a restaurant which offers themed menus such as Dracula's tomato soup and fairly average food.

14 Not all the themed food given to the tourists on the hunt for Count Dracula is poor. One of the best and most exciting meals of the holiday was at the Count Dracula Club in Bucharest. Once the children got over the fear of the stuffed bears and stags on the walls and dog head skulls hanging from the ceiling, the food was fantastic — thick vegetable soup, polenta with stuffed cabbage leaves. The children drank blood orange juice and feasted on thick stew. Down in the cellar was the coffin, with the waiters dressed like vampires and acting for all they were worth.

15 Away from the crypts was hot summer sunshine: we swam in outdoor swimming pools and visited spas with bubbling warm salt lakes. We felt Romania would be a good place to revisit when the boys were older and could hike and camp in the Carpathian wilderness. The most memorable part of our visit to Romania was staying with a delightful family in Sighisoara who loved the children and treated them with kindness as they helped feed their chickens and cook special apple cake.

16 But if we leave the return visit too long things will have changed dramatically. A DraculaLand theme park is planned to be built by a German or American corporation in medieval Sighisoara next year.

17 Local opinion is divided. On the one hand, there is the desire for tourist money and on the other the realisation that the theme park will change the character of the small town forever. If the cobbled streets are lined with fast food chains offering "stakeburgers" and garlic bread — Dracula will be turning in his grave.

Adapted from an article by
Catriona Marchant

[*END OF PASSAGE*]

[BLANK PAGE]

FOR OFFICIAL USE

G

Total Mark

0860/404

NATIONAL QUALIFICATIONS 2003

TUESDAY, 6 MAY
1.00 PM – 1.50 PM

ENGLISH
General Level
Reading
Questions

Fill in these boxes and read what is printed below.

Full name of centre

Town

Forename(s)

Surname

Date of birth
Day Month Year

Scottish candidate number

Number of seat

NB Before leaving the examination room you must give this booklet to the invigilator. If you do not, you may lose all the marks for this paper.

SCOTTISH QUALIFICATIONS AUTHORITY

Marks

QUESTIONS

Write your answers in the spaces provided.

Look at Paragraph 1.

1. **In what two ways** does the writer create a frightening atmosphere in the opening sentence? 2 1 0

(i) ______

(ii) ______

2. Explain fully what the writer suggests by using the word "flickering" when describing the candle. 2 1 0

This suggests that it could go out at any time, making the atmosphere even more tense as the candle is the only source of light.

Look at Paragraph 2.

3. "My three brave boys"

Explain fully why this expression might be considered to be surprising. 2 1 0

As, in the discription of the boys it explains that they are scared there for Not being Brave.

4. **Explain in your own words** how Matthew had been treating his brothers. 2 ■ 0

Matthew being the oldest began to make fun of his younger Brother when he was most scared & vonarable, but later it changes & Matthew aslo becomes scared.

Look at Paragraph 3.

5. **Give two pieces of evidence** which suggest that Bram Stoker wrote the novel *Dracula* more than one hundred years ago. 2 1 0

(i) The word Victorian is used suggesting long ago.

(ii) ______

6. Why does the writer use dashes in Paragraph 3? 2 ■ 0

TO separate the important pieces of information.

PAGE TOTAL

Look at Paragraph 4.

Marks

7. "Downstairs was Count Dracula's coffin in a narrow vault, the walls painted with the dramatic scenes"

In what ways does the writer convey the "dramatic scenes" in the vault?

By using words like narrow this creates the scence of clostraphobia. The writer also gets his idea of the colour of the wall across in a very dramatic way, by saying that they were smeared with the blood of his victims.

2 1 0

8. What effect does the writer create by using the expression "So far on our Romanian holiday the only blood-sucking had been from the mosquitoes"?

This expression creates a minute of ~~reliefe~~ relife for the reader, it is a break from the grusem discriptions of the post sentences.

2 ■ 0

9. **In your own words** explain fully why their father was sent down first.

To see if the 3 young boys could cope with the fear when going downstairs.

2 1 0

Look at Paragraphs 5, 6 and 7.

10. **Write down an expression** which shows that Matthew did not complete the tour.

Matthew decided he would opt from the tour.

2 ■ 0

11. **In your own words** what is the writer's attitude to the various goods for sale in the hotel lobby?

She thinks that the gift shop being filled with things associated with dracula took the dignatey from the place she expreces this by saying it is tacky

2 ■ 0

12. **In your own words** what is the writer's opinion of the setting of the Hotel Castel Dracula?

The writer is impressed with the authenticness of the castle as it is obveously not the real one.

2 ■ 0

13. Why does the writer place the word "castle" in inverted commas?

She is enphosising that it is not an actual castle but a building resembaling one.

2 ■ 0

PAGE TOTAL

Marks

Look at Paragraphs 8 and 9.

14. What was the real name of the original Dracula?

~~Count Dracula~~. Prince vlad Tepes

2 ■ 0

15. Explain **in your own words** how Romania benefits from "this confusion between fiction and history".

AS many tourists are drawn in to the country by the mith of dracula ~~that go into Romania~~

2 1 0

Look at Paragraph 10.

16. What contrasting impressions does the writer give of Bran Castle?

some features of the castle seem imposing and fearful and others cosy & welcoming.

2 1 0

Look at Paragraphs 11, 12 and 13.

17. "He gained more smiles and laughs than any signs of horror"

Give two reasons why Matthew was an unconvincing vampire.

He had cut out paper fangs ~~that~~ not Life like,

The time of day was sunny & not scary atmosphere so it was a bad time to scare people

2 1 0

18. What does the expression "fiery concoction" suggest about the Dracula's Kiss drink?

AS it contained lots of alcohol.

2 1 0

PAGE TOTAL

Marks

Look at Paragraph 14.

19. (*a*) **In your own words explain how** the boys felt at the start of their visit to the Count Dracula Club. **Why** did they feel this way?

They were very scared at the begining but once they had realised the fact that it was fiction they had a great time eating the groosemly named foods.

2 1 0

(*b*) **Write down an expression** which clearly shows that the boys changed their attitude to the visit.

once the children got over the fact.

2 ■ 0

Look at Paragraphs 15, 16 and 17.

20. What kind of holiday in Romania might the writer consider in the future?

A nature (out doors) holiday in Romania.

2 1 0

21. (*a*) How does the writer feel about the changes planned for the tourist industry in Romania?

She does not want the theme park to go up as she says that they cant leave it long (meaning there holiday).

2 ■ 0

(*b*) Explain **in your own words** how the local people feel about the planned changes.

They have mixed feeling one it the money that will be gained & the other is that it will change the small towns "characteristics". (how it looks.)

2 1 0

(*c*) "Dracula will be turning in his grave."

Why does the writer finish off the final sentence in this way?

As she means to be ironic by saying this because dracula sleeps in his coffin.

2 1 0

[Turn over for Question 22 on *Page six*

PAGE TOTAL

Marks

Think about the passage as a whole.

22. "Catriona Marchant and her children discover that Dracula has a big stake in Romania's tourist industry."

Explain fully what is appropriate about this sub-title.

As this is what can kill dracula there for it is associated with dracula so the sub-title goes well with the story.

2 1 0

[*END OF QUESTION PAPER*]

PAGE TOTAL

[BLANK PAGE]

F

0860/401

NATIONAL QUALIFICATIONS 2004

WEDNESDAY, 5 MAY
10.35 AM – 11.25 AM

ENGLISH
STANDARD GRADE
Foundation Level
Reading
Text

Read carefully the passage overleaf. It will help if you read it twice. When you have done so, answer the questions. Use the spaces provided in the Question/Answer booklet.

SCOTTISH QUALIFICATIONS AUTHORITY

In this extract the narrator and his brother are on an overnight camping and hunting trip when something unusual happens.

1 At some point I drifted off to sleep and when I woke I thought it was dawn. Then I realised the pale light coming through the canvas was moonlight. I was absolutely alert, and tense. Something had wakened me. I lay there, hardly daring to breathe. Then I heard a whisper, a low hiss of a whisper, outside the tent. It was calling my name.

2 Somebody was out there. My brother was breathing gently beside me, fast asleep. I simply listened. I don't know what I thought. I felt no fear, but still I was amazed to feel the tears trickling slowly down over my ears, as I lay staring upwards.

3 The whisper came again, my name. It seemed to be coming from about where the fire was.

4 Very carefully, partly not to waken my brother, partly not to let the voice know I was listening, I sat up, leaned forward, and tried to peep through the laced-up door of the tent. By holding the edges of the flaps slightly apart, I could see a tiny dot of red glow still in our campfire. Everything out there was drenched in a grey, misty light.

5 Somebody was standing beside the fire.

6 It was a person and yet I got the impression it was somehow not a person. Or it was a very small person. It looked like a small old woman, with a peculiar bonnet on her head and a long shawl. That was my impression. As I stared with all my might, trying to make out something definite, this figure drifted backwards into the shade of the trees. But the whisper came again:

7 "Come out. Quickly. There's been an accident."

8 I immediately knew it must be somebody from the farm. Surely it was the farmer's little old mother. That was how she knew we were here. The farmer had fallen down a well, or down a loft ladder, or a mad cow had crushed his ribs. Or he'd simply tumbled downstairs going to get his old mother a cup of tea because she couldn't sleep.

9 Something stopped me waking my brother. What I really wanted was to find out more. Who was this person? What was the accident? Anyway, it was my name that had been called. It must be me that was specially needed. I could come back and tell my brother later. Most of all, I wanted to see who this was.

10 I had gone to sleep in my clothes, to keep warm and for a quick start. So now I pulled on my boots. I unlaced the tent door at the bottom and crawled out. The grass was cold and soaking under my hands.

11 "Hurry," came the whisper from under the trees. "Hurry, hurry."

12 It seems strange, that I felt no fear. I was so sure that it was somebody from the farm, that I thought of no other possibility. Only huge curiosity, and excitement. Also, I felt quite important suddenly.

13 I went toward the voice, staring into the dark shade. The moon was past full but very hard and white. I wanted to get into the shade quickly, where I wouldn't be so visible.

14 But now the voice came again, from further up the wood. Yes, the voice was climbing towards the farm.

15 "Hurry," it kept saying. "Hurry up."

16 Beneath the trees, the slope was clear and grassy, without brambles or undergrowth. Easy going but steep, with that tough, slippery grass.

17 As I climbed, the voice went ahead. Very soon, I would see through the top of the wood. The bright night sky was piled with brilliant masses of snowy cloud, beyond the dark tree stems. I glimpsed the black outline now and again, the funny bonnet, climbing ahead, bobbing between the trees.

18 "Are you coming?" came the whisper again. "This way."

19 I saw her shape in the gap of the wall, clear against those snowy clouds. Then she had gone through it. It was now, as I came up towards the gap, sometimes grasping grass to help myself upwards, that I saw something else, bouncing and scrabbling under the wall, in a clear patch of moonlight.

20 A great slab of stone had fallen. Beside it sat a well-grown fox cub, staring up at me, panting. As I took this in, the cub suddenly started again, tugging and bouncing, jerking and scrabbling, without a sound, till again it crouched there, staring up at me, its mouth wide open, its tongue dangling, panting.

21 I could see now that it was trapped by one hind leg and its tail. They were pinned to the ground under the corner of the big slab.

22 The smell was overpowering, thick, choking, almost liquid, as if concentrated liquid scent had been poured over me, soaking my clothes and hands. I knew the smell of fox – the smell of frightened fox.

23 Then I looked up and saw the figure out there in the field, only five yards away, watching me. More than ever I could see it was a little old woman, with her very thin legs and her funny bonnet and shawl. She did not seem to be wanting me to go to the farm. She had brought me to this fox cub. She was probably some eccentric old lady who never slept, or slept only by day and spent the night roaming the hillsides, talking to owls and befriending foxes. She would have seen our camp. Probably some of those tracks had been hers, brushed through the dew around our tent. Now she had found the trapped cub, and not being strong enough to lift the slab, she had come to us. She wanted me to lift the slab and free the cub. She had not called my brother because she thought he might kill it. She must have watched us, and heard him speak my name.

24 My first thought was to catch the cub and keep it alive. But how could I hold it and at the same time lift the slab? It was a desperate, ferocious little thing. I could have wrapped it in my jersey, knotting the arms round it. But I didn't think of that. As I put my fingers under the other corner of the slab, the cub snapped its teeth at me and hissed like a cat, then struggled again, jerking to free itself.

25 With all my strength I was just able to budge the slab a fraction. But it was enough. As the slab shifted, the cub scrabbled and was gone – off down the wood like a rocket.

26 I looked up at the old lady, and this was my next surprise. The bare, close-cropped, moonlit field was empty. I walked out to where she had been. The whole wide field, under the great bare sky of moonlight, all made much brighter by that great bulging heap of snowy, silvery clouds, was empty. Not even a sheep. Absolutely nothing.

Adapted from *Deadfall* by Ted Hughes

[*END OF PASSAGE*]

[BLANK PAGE]

FOR OFFICIAL USE

F

Total Mark

0860/402

NATIONAL QUALIFICATIONS 2004

WEDNESDAY, 5 MAY
10.35 AM – 11.25 AM

ENGLISH STANDARD GRADE

Foundation Level Reading Questions

Fill in these boxes and read what is printed below.

Full name of centre

Town

Forename(s)

Surname

Date of birth
Day Month Year

Scottish candidate number

Number of seat

NB Before leaving the examination room you must give this booklet to the invigilator. If you do not, you may lose all the marks for this paper.

SCOTTISH QUALIFICATIONS AUTHORITY

Marks

QUESTIONS

Write your answers in the spaces provided.

Look at Paragraph 1.

1. **Write down an expression** which shows that the boy was unsure of when he had fallen asleep.

   ______________________________ 2

2. What made the boy think that he had slept until dawn?

   ______________________________ 2

3. What did the boy hear and what was unusual about it?

   ______________________________ 2 1

4. **Write down two expressions** from Paragraph 1 which show how the boy was feeling. 2 1

   (i) ______________________________

   (ii) ______________________________

Look at Paragraphs 2 and 3.

5. "Somebody was out there." (Paragraph 2)

   Why does the writer use this short sentence here?

   ____

   ______________________________ 2 1

6. Why was the boy's brother unaware of what was happening?

   ______________________________ 2

Look at Paragraph 4.

7. **Write down two reasons** why the boy moved very carefully inside the tent. 2 1

   (i) ______________________________

   (ii) ______________________________

PAGE TOTAL

Marks

8. What was **the first thing** the boy saw when he peeped through the tent flap? 2 1 0

9. "Everything out there was drenched in a grey, misty light."

Why does the writer use the word "drenched"? 2 1 0

Look at Paragraphs 5 to 8.

10. **Write down three things** the boy noticed about the person standing beside the fire. 2 1 0

(i)

(ii)

(iii)

11. **Write down an expression** from Paragraph 6 which tells you that the boy was concentrating on the figure. 2 ■ 0

12. What important information did the figure give to the boy? 2 ■ 0

Look at Paragraphs 9 to 11.

13. **Write down three reasons** the boy gives for not wakening his brother. 2 1 0

(i)

(ii)

(iii)

14. Why was it possible for the boy to get ready so quickly? 2 ■ 0

PAGE TOTAL

Marks

Look at Paragraphs 12 to 14.

15. **Write down two expressions** which tell you the boy was certain that it was someone from the farm. 2 1 0

(i) ______

(ii) ______

16. **In your own words** what reason does the boy give for getting into the shade quickly?

______

______ 2 1 0

Look at Paragraphs 15 to 18.

17. **Write down an expression** which helps to make the meaning of "glimpsed" clear.

______ 2 ■ 0

Look at Paragraphs 19 to 22.

18. In what **two different ways** does the writer make the trapped fox cub's panic clear in Paragraph 20? 2 1 0

(i) ______

(ii) ______

19. **In your own words** what was the boy's reaction to the smell of the fox?

______

______ 2 1 0

Look at Paragraph 23.

20. What did the boy now realise about the little old lady's purpose in leading him there?

______ 2 ■ 0

21. **Write down the word** from Paragraph 23 which the boy uses to describe the little old lady's odd behaviour.

______ 2 ■ 0

PAGE TOTAL

Marks

22. **Write down two reasons** why she had chosen the boy to rescue the cub. **2 1 0**

(i) ______________________________

(ii) ______________________________

Look at Paragraphs 24 to 26.

23. ". . . ferocious little thing." (Paragraph 24)

Write down two expressions from later in the paragraph which develop this idea. **2 1 0**

(i) ______________________________

(ii) ______________________________

24. Why does the writer use the expression "off down the wood like a rocket" to describe the cub's movements?

____

______________________________ **2 1 0**

Think about the passage as a whole.

25. Who do you think the old lady was? **Using evidence from the passage** give a reason for your answer.

____

____

______________________________ **2 1 0**

[*END OF QUESTION PAPER*]

PAGE TOTAL

FOR OFFICIAL USE

p2	
p3	
p4	
p5	
TOTAL MARK	

[BLANK PAGE]

G

0860/403

NATIONAL QUALIFICATIONS 2004

WEDNESDAY, 5 MAY
1.00 PM – 1.50 PM

ENGLISH STANDARD GRADE
General Level
Reading
Text

Read carefully the passage overleaf. It will help if you read it twice. When you have done so, answer the questions. Use the spaces provided in the Question/Answer booklet.

SAB 0860/403 6/71420

Pucker Way to Kiss a Hummingbird

Mark Carwardine puts on lipstick in Arizona for a wild encounter.

SUMMER SPECTACLE:
Thousands of hummingbirds arrive in Arizona every year

1 There's a rather embarrassing tradition in wildlife circles in certain parts of Arizona. Visiting naturalists are encouraged to try to "kiss" a wild hummingbird.

2 This is more of a challenge for men than it is for women – mainly because it involves wearing lots of red lipstick. A dress and high heels are optional, but the redder and thicker the lipstick the better. Hummingbirds drink nectar from flowers that are often bright red and have learned to associate this particular colour with food. They mistake your mouth for one of their favourite plants – at least, that's the theory.

3 Which is how I found myself high in the mountains of South-East Arizona, with puckered lips pointing sky-ward and a crowd of bemused onlookers egging me on.

4 My home for a couple of days was Beatty's Guest Ranch near the Mexico border. Run by Tom and Edith Beatty, the ranch is nearly 6,000ft above sea level, nestling between two enormous peaks, with spectacular views down the valley to the desert below.

5 According to the South-Eastern Arizona Bird Observatory, it is the hottest hummingbird-watching spot in the state. Thousands of "hummers" arrive in April and May and stay until early October. No fewer than 15 different species are found here on a regular basis.

6 Dozens of special hummingbird feeders, looking like upside-down jam jars, are dotted around the ranch. Hanging from trees, bushes, fences and buildings they are full of a simple magic potion (four parts water, one part white sugar) similar to the nectar of hummingbird flowers. Tom and Edith keep the feeders topped up, getting through a mind-boggling 550 2lb bags of sugar in a typical year.

7 There were two feeders outside my bedroom window in the turn-of-the-century self-catering cabin on the forest edge (not a good place to stay if you've seen *Friday The 13th* or *The Blair Witch Project*, but idyllic in every other sense).

8 I will never forget pulling back the curtains on the first morning. There were hummingbirds everywhere, whizzing backwards and forwards past the window like demented bees. Sometimes they paused in front of the sugar-water to feed, either perching or hovering with the immaculate precision of experienced helicopter pilots.

9 Apparently, it's possible to see as many as ten species at the ranch in just half an hour. But even when they stayed still for more than a few moments I had no idea which was which. As they moved around, their colours changed in relation to the angle of the sun. Bird identification is hard enough at the best of times, but this was ridiculous.

10 Take a male hummingbird, for example. When you look at it face-to-face its throat is a fiery scarlet red. But as it turns away the colour shifts – first to orange, then yellow, then blackish-brown and then green. Try identifying that in a hurry, before it turns

into a blur and helicopters away.

11 I think there were Anna's hummingbirds, black-chinned, broad billed, blue-throated, magnificent, red and violet-crowned that morning, but I'm not entirely sure. Later, I asked other bird-watchers about similar-looking hummers around "their" feeding station, but they weren't sure either. I left them bickering over the difference between the sapphire blue throat of a broad-bill and the cobalt blue throat of a blue-throat.

12 The biological advantage of changing colour is that the birds can control the way they look. If a male wants to impress a female he shows his best side, but if he wants to hide from a predator he merely turns away and almost disappears among the greenery.

13 According to Sheri Williamson, hummingbird expert and co-founder of the South-Eastern Arizona Bird Observatory, you can tell them apart by the sound of their wings. Broad-tailed hummingbirds, for example, have a metallic trill to their wingbeats, while male black-chinned hummingbirds make a dull, flat whine.

14 Sheri took me to see a hummingbird in the hand. There's a ringing station, or banding station as they call it in the States, at nearby Sierra Vista. It's open to the public and every weekend the observatory staff rig up a mist-net trap with a tasty-looking sugar-water feeder in the middle. Whenever a hummingbird dares an investigatory hover, a burly member of the observatory team rushes forward, waving his arms around, and ushers the unfortunate bird inside.

15 We caught lots of hummingbirds that day. One was a female black-chinned that squealed when she was caught. It was hard to tell whether this was out of fear or anger ("How could I, so fleet of wing, be caught by this enormous fool?"). We found her abdomen distended with an enormous egg, which Sheri guessed would be laid before nightfall.

16 For a brief moment, I actually held the delicate bundle of feathers in my hand, and was so nervous about squeezing too hard that she escaped. After hovering above us for a moment, she made a bee-line for the bushes.

17 Hovering hummingbirds draw crowds of naturalists from all over the world to South-East Arizona, but hovering does have one major drawback. Pound for pound, beating your wings 70 times per second uses more energy than any other activity in the animal kingdom. Living life in the fast lane means hummingbirds need a continuous supply of fuel.

18 A typical hummingbird eats around half its own weight in energy-rich nectar every day. To do that it has to keep others away from its favourite foodplants. I spent many hours watching them battle it out at feeding stations. Far from being all sweetness and light, they are little fighter pilots. If they were the size of ravens it wouldn't be safe to walk in the woods.

19 Before I left, there was one thing I had to do. Dutifully, I put on bright red lipstick, took a mouthful of sugar-water, sat back, puckered my lips . . . and waited. Within 30 seconds two hummingbirds came to investigate. Others soon followed.

20 I sat there for an eternity not daring to move. No hummingbird actually drank sugar-water from my mouth (who can blame them?), but several did hover so close I could feel their wingbeats against my cheeks.

21 Strangely, the encounter was every bit as impressive as rubbing shoulders with mountain gorillas in the wilds of Africa or performing slow-motion underwater ballets with dolphins in the Bahamas.

22 Even better, my biggest worry came to nothing – the red lipstick wiped off.

(*Adapted from an article by Mark Carwardine*)

[*END OF PASSAGE*]

[BLANK PAGE]

FOR OFFICIAL USE

G

Total Mark

0860/404

NATIONAL QUALIFICATIONS 2004

WEDNESDAY, 5 MAY
1.00 PM – 1.50 PM

ENGLISH
STANDARD GRADE
General Level
Reading
Questions

Fill in these boxes and read what is printed below.

Full name of centre

Town

Forename(s)

Surname

Date of birth
Day Month Year

Scottish candidate number

Number of seat

NB Before leaving the examination room you must give this booklet to the invigilator. If you do not, you may lose all the marks for this paper.

SCOTTISH QUALIFICATIONS AUTHORITY

Marks

QUESTIONS

Write your answers in the spaces provided.

Look at Paragraphs 1 and 2.

1. **Write down a word** from Paragraph 1 that suggests naturalists might be reluctant to kiss a hummingbird.

   ______________________________ 2 ■ 0

2. Why are the hummingbirds attracted to someone wearing bright red lipstick?

   ____

   ______________________________ 2 1 0

3. Why do you think the writer uses the word "theory" in Paragraph 2?

   ______________________________ 2 ■ 0

Look at Paragraphs 3 and 4.

4. Where **exactly** did the writer first meet the hummingbirds?

   ____

   ______________________________ 2 1 0

Look at Paragraphs 5 and 6.

5. Thousands of "hummers" (Paragraph 5)

   Why has the writer put the word "hummers" in inverted commas?

   ____

   ______________________________ 2 ■ 0

PAGE TOTAL

Marks

6. "Hanging from trees, bushes, fences and buildings they are full of a simple magic potion . . . flowers." (Paragraph 6)

Identify and comment on the effect of **two features** of the structure of this sentence.

(i) ____

____ 2 1 0

(ii) ____

____ 2 1 0

7. **Write down an expression** from Paragraph 6 which tells you that the writer is surprised by the amount of sugar used.

____ 2 ■ 0

Look at Paragraphs 7 and 8.

8. What do the expressions "whizzing" and "like demented bees" tell you about the movement of the hummingbirds?

____

____ 2 1 0

9. **Write down an expression** which shows that the writer admires the flying skills of the hummingbird.

____ 2 ■ 0

Look at Paragraphs 9 and 10.

10. **In your own words** write down **two** reasons why the writer found bird identification "ridiculous". 2 1 0

(i) ____

(ii) ____

PAGE TOTAL

Marks

Look at Paragraphs 11 and 12.

11. What does the writer's use of the word "bickering" tell you about his attitude to the bird watchers?

____________________ 2

12. In your own words give **two** reasons why hummingbirds change their colour. 2 1

(i) ____________________

(ii) ____________________

Look at Paragraphs 13 to 15.

13. How does Sheri Williamson tell the difference between hummingbirds?

____

____________________ 2 1

14. Comment on the writer's use of the expression "hummingbird in the hand".

____

____________________ 2 1

15. "Whenever a hummingbird dares an investigatory hover, a burly member of the observatory team rushes forward, waving his arms around" (Paragraph 14)

How does this description create effective contrasts?

(i) ____________________ 2

(ii) ____________________ 2

Look at Paragraph 16.

16. What does the expression "I actually held" tell you about how the writer felt when he held the hummingbird?

____

____________________ 2

PAGE TOTAL

Marks

Look at Paragraphs 17 and 18.

17. "Living life in the fast lane means hummingbirds need a continuous supply of fuel." (Paragraph 17)

Explain the effectiveness of this image.

2 1 0

18. **In your own words**, what **two** new impressions does the writer give of the hummingbird in Paragraph 18?

2 1 0

Look at Paragraphs 19 to 22.

19. "Dutifully, I put on bright red lipstick . . . puckered my lips . . . and waited." (Paragraph 19)

Identify and comment on any **one feature** of structure **or** punctuation in this sentence.

2 1 0

20. **Write down an expression** from Paragraph 20 which tells us the writer felt he waited for a long time.

2 ■ 0

21. **In your own words** what does the writer's use of the word "Strangely" tell you about his reaction to the encounter with the hummingbirds?

2 ■ 0

[Turn over for Questions 22 and 23 on *Page six*

PAGE TOTAL

Marks

Think about the passage as a whole.

22. From the passage **write down an example** of the writer's use of humour.

Explain why it is effective.

2 1 0

23. Overall how do you think the writer feels about his experience with the humming-birds?

Support your answer by referring to the passage.

2 1 0

[*END OF QUESTION PAPER*]

PAGE TOTAL

[BLANK PAGE]

F

0860/401

NATIONAL QUALIFICATIONS 2005

WEDNESDAY, 4 MAY
10.35 AM – 11.25 AM

ENGLISH STANDARD GRADE

Foundation Level
Reading
Text

Read carefully the passage overleaf. It will help if you read it twice. When you have done so, answer the questions. Use the spaces provided in the Question/Answer booklet.

SCOTTISH QUALIFICATIONS AUTHORITY

1 When he first woke up, Pete Smeaton was sure he was still dreaming.

2 Then he opened his eyes and knew that it had really happened. He was lying in a sleeping bag on the floor of a room in his new home. A home he had never set eyes on before.

3 And Jenny was crying.

4 At least some things never changed.

5 Pete sat up stiffly and looked around. Whatever room he was in was furnished with nothing but packing cartons stacked one on top of the other. He couldn't tell if the room was large or small because all he could see were boxes, labelled in his mother's hasty scrawl:

Kitchen, My room, Hall, Pete, Jenny.

6 He remembered the hurried squeak of the marker pen on the boxes as the carrier waited to transport them up from London. That was just yesterday.

7 Even muffled by packing cartons, Jenny's cry was shrill and piercing. Pete groaned and flopped back on his sleeping bag. He closed his eyes and put his hands over his ears. The crying grew louder. Pete opened one eye, as Jenny was shoved into his arms.

8 "Take her, will you, so I can at least go to the toilet on my own. If I put her down she'll be sick. This new place is giving her the heebie-jeebies. She was up all night."

9 Pete's mother left him with the hot, open-mouthed bundle that was his baby sister. Three months old and more hassle than twenty Petes had ever been, according to Mrs Smeaton.

10 Pete stared into the tiny, furious face.

11 "Hel–lo noisy," he said slowly. Secretly, he loved the feeling of Jenny when he held her although he would never admit that out loud to anyone. No way!

12 Hearing Pete's voice, Jenny stopped crying instantly. Pete felt her body relax in his arms.

13 "Why d'you always stop crying for me, you little monkey?" Pete whispered on Jenny's downy head. "You should give Mum a break."

14 Fitting Jenny expertly in the crook of one arm, Pete levered himself up from the floor.

15 "C'mon let's see what this place is like, Jenny. Time to explore."

16 The floorboards felt rough and chilly under Pete's feet. Snuggling Jenny close he went out into the hallway.

17 "Must have slept in the lounge," Pete figured. He was downstairs and the only other room on this floor was a large square kitchen with a small scullery. Beyond lay a wild-looking garden.

18 "It's a jungle out there, Jenny," said Pete in an American accent. "Better wait till I'm armed before I investigate."

19 Upstairs, on the half landing of the house there was a bathroom and one huge empty bedroom. The morning sun streamed through its emptiness illuminating the specks of dust which danced in such numbers that the room appeared in soft focus.

20 Pete stood in the centre of this room and knew that he wanted it to be his. It was at least three times the size of his old bedroom in London.

21 Quickly, he planned where he would put his books and lean his guitar. His bed would fit perfectly in that corner over there, and if his desk fitted under the window he'd be able to look outside and daydream while he was supposed to be doing his homework.

22 There'd be enough room for all his friends to stay overnight if they brought their sleeping bags.

23 "We could have a midnight feast and make up all those songs that drive Mum mad and . . ."

24 Pete was whispering excitedly to Jenny. Then he remembered where he was now:

25 "What an idiot. What friends?" he said bitterly to Jenny. "Don't know anyone here, do I? Never even heard of Clydebank before in my life. Don't even know what bloomin' school I'll be going to."

26 Pete stared into Jenny's blue unblinking eyes.

27 "You're lucky. Bet we'll be back in London by the time you need any friends. How am I going to meet anyone here?"

28 Pete leaned his forehead despondently on the glass and stared down at the garden. It really did look like a jungle. An expanse of unruly grasses weaved before Pete, reaching down to a ramshackle brick outbuilding. Beyond that, the boundary of the garden was drawn by a row of mature trees and bushes.

29 "It's huge," thought Pete, who had never lived in a house with a garden before. He had to admit—grudgingly—that this garden looked big enough for a decent game of football. It was his birthday next week. Maybe he'd ask for goalposts instead of that portable CD player he had his eye on.

30 Pete gazed out the window and saw himself running out onto the grass heading a crowd of boys:

31 "Good pass, Pete."

32 "Here, over to me, Pete."

33 "Yeah, nice one, Pete."

34 "Pete, Pete."

35 "Pete? Where on earth have you gone?"

36 Mrs Smeaton's irritation interrupted his daydream.

37 "What you doing with her now? It's all dusty up here." She shuddered, "Ugh! And chilly."

38 Mrs Smeaton yanked Jenny from Pete's arms. She was asleep, a smug little smile playing over her lips.

39 "Now look what you've done," Mrs Smeaton's voice rose in frustration. "I wanted to feed her first."

40 Pete shrugged, "Sorry, Mum. She was awake two minutes ago. Honest." He was going to add, "Got the magic touch, haven't I?" but something about his mum's pinched face and tired, shaky voice made him stop. She looked as though she was going to start crying again. He really hated that. Never could get used to it, even though she cried all the time these days. Her tears made Pete feel panicky and scared.

41 Quickly he asked, "Mum, can I have this room if you and Dad don't want it?"

42 "Do what you like," snapped the answer. "Won't make any difference to me. I don't sleep these days with this one yammering all the time. Someone in this family might as well use one of the bedrooms to get some rest."

 [Turn over

43 The bitterness in his mother's voice made Pete wince. He stood at the door of his new room watching her slump wearily downstairs with Jenny in her arms. There was a horrible tight feeling inside his chest.

44 By the time Mrs Smeaton had reached the bottom stair, Jenny was wailing.

45 "Oh, for goodness' sake," Pete heard his mother sigh, as she carried Jenny through to the kitchen, slamming the door behind her so hard that the whole house shook.

46 Then the wailing became louder. And louder still. It turned into sobbing. Huge, uncontrollable sobbing. Pete stood with his hand on the door knob and listened.

47 "Mum?"

48 Pete was more taken aback by the power of the crying than by the crying itself. Surely it wasn't Jenny? It was much too powerful. Whoever was crying was much closer than the kitchen downstairs. And it sounded like a child. Right next to Pete.

Adapted from *Think Me Back* by Catherine Forde

[*END OF PASSAGE*]

FOR OFFICIAL USE

F

Total Mark

0860/402

NATIONAL QUALIFICATIONS 2005

WEDNESDAY, 4 MAY
10.35 AM – 11.25 AM

ENGLISH STANDARD GRADE

Foundation Level Reading Questions

Fill in these boxes and read what is printed below.

Full name of centre

Town

Forename(s)

Surname

Date of birth

Day Month Year

Scottish candidate number

Number of seat

NB Before leaving the examination room you must give this booklet to the invigilator. If you do not, you may lose all the marks for this paper.

SCOTTISH QUALIFICATIONS AUTHORITY

Marks

QUESTIONS

Write your answers in the spaces provided.

Look at Paragraphs 1 to 4.

1. What was Pete's first thought when he woke up?

2 ■ 0

2. What important event had just happened in Pete's life?

2 ■ 0

3. "At least some things never changed."

What does this sentence suggest?

2 ■ 0

Look at Paragraphs 5 and 6.

4. "mother's hasty scrawl:"

(*a*) Give **two** reasons why the writer uses this expression to describe the writing on the boxes. 2 1 0

(i)

(ii)

(*b*) **Write down one word** from Paragraph 6 which continues this idea.

2 ■ 0

Look at Paragraph 7.

5. **Write down two words** which describe Jenny's cry.

2 1 0

PAGE TOTAL

Marks

6. How did Pete feel about Jenny's crying?

2 ■ 0

Look at Paragraphs 8 to 10.

7. **Give two reasons** why Pete's mother asked him to hold the baby. 2 1 0

(i)

(ii)

8. **Write down an expression** which tells you that Pete had been an easier baby than Jenny.

2 ■ 0

Look at Paragraphs 11 to 13.

9. Look at the final sentence of Paragraph 11.

How does the writer show Pete's strong feelings through

(i) sentence structure?

(ii) punctuation?

2 1 0

10. How did hearing Pete's voice affect Jenny?

2 1 0

11. **Write down the expression** which shows that Pete felt sorry for his mum.

2 ■ 0

[Turn over

PAGE TOTAL

Marks

Look at Paragraphs 14 to 19.

12. **Write down one word** which shows that Pete was good at looking after his little sister.

2 ■ 0

13. "Snuggling Jenny close" (Paragraph 16)

Why did Pete do this?

2 1 0

Look at Paragraphs 20 to 25.

14. Write down any **three** things which Pete liked about the room.

2 1 0

(i)

(ii)

(iii)

15. "We could have a midnight feast and make up all those songs that drive Mum mad and . . ." (Paragraph 23)

Why did Pete not finish what he was saying?

2 1 0

Look at Paragraphs 26 to 28.

16. **Write down the word** which shows that Pete thought there was no hope of having friends in his new home.

2 ■ 0

PAGE TOTAL

Marks

17. **Write down three expressions** which tell you that the garden had not been looked after. 2 1 0

(i) ________________________________

(ii) ________________________________

(iii) ________________________________

Look at Paragraphs 29 to 34.

18. While daydreaming about the garden Pete imagined himself to be:

a football player ☐

a football referee ☐

a football fan ☐ 2 ■ 0

Tick (✓) the correct box.

Look at Paragraphs 35 to 40.

19. "Mrs Smeaton's irritation interrupted his daydream." (Paragraph 36)

Write down two words from later **in this section of the passage** which develop the idea that Mrs Smeaton was angry.

☐ ☐ 2 1 0

20. What **three** things stopped Pete from continuing to answer his mother back? 2 1 0

(i) ________________________________

(ii) ________________________________

(iii) ________________________________

Look at Paragraphs 41 to 48.

21. "Mum, can I have this room if you and Dad don't want it?" (Paragraph 41)

Why did Pete ask his mum this question at this time?

________________________________ 2 ■ 0

[Turn over for Questions 22 to 24 on *Page six*

PAGE TOTAL

Marks

22. Write down three expressions which the writer uses to show that Pete's mother was still angry. **2 1 0**

(i) ______________________________

(ii) ______________________________

(iii) ______________________________

23. "Surely it wasn't Jenny?" (Paragraph 48)

What **two** things made Pete think this? **2 1 0**

(i) ______________________________

(ii) ______________________________

Think about the passage as a whole.

24. Tick (✓) **two words** which you think best describe Pete's character.

Give evidence from the passage to support your choices. **2 1 0**

Caring ☐

Imaginative ☐

Moody ☐

Sensitive ☐

(i) ______________________________

____

(ii) ______________________________

____

[*END OF QUESTION PAPER*]

FOR OFFICIAL USE

p2	
p3	
p4	
p5	
p6	
TOTAL MARK	

[BLANK PAGE]

[BLANK PAGE]

G

0860/403

NATIONAL QUALIFICATIONS 2005

WEDNESDAY, 4 MAY
1.00 PM – 1.50 PM

ENGLISH STANDARD GRADE

General Level
Reading
Text

Read carefully the passage overleaf. It will help if you read it twice. When you have done so, answer the questions. Use the spaces provided in the Question/Answer booklet.

SCOTTISH QUALIFICATIONS AUTHORITY

Dazzled by the Stars

Our love affair with fame may be bad for our health, according to new research. **John Harlow** reports on "celebrity worship syndrome".

1 Under her bed Katherine Hicks keeps six years of yellowing newspaper clippings about the former pop band Boyzone, and 70 videos of their performances. There might have been more if her attention had not moved on to Westlife, another pop sensation.

2 In one year she has spent £3,000 to watch Westlife perform 17 times, and is such a regular concert fan that she believes the band now recognise her as an acquaintance, if not a friend.

3 She has fixed her sights on a new star: David Sneddon, first winner of the television show Fame Academy. She cornered Sneddon at two television appearances, though it is early days in her "acquaintance" with him. Yet she felt forced to defend him indignantly against a TV presenter who, she thought, had not shown Sneddon sufficient respect.

4 Hicks is no deluded young teen: she is a 28-year-old electrical engineer. But she freely admits to an "addiction" to the latest musical sensations. "I have an obsessive nature. Anything I do is full-on, but it has never caused me problems," she said last week. "I don't do anything I cannot afford, and I don't ring in sick at work to get time off."

5 She is no stalker or obsessive; she is just "fascinated by the real personas of these people". Though she likens her behaviour to an "addiction rather than an illness", she sees nothing odd in it.

6 "Other people think I am ill or sad," she said, "but I am not missing out on anything."

7 Psychologists, who are taking an increasing interest in the effects of celebrity culture, might disagree. As Anglo-American research published last week reveals, our relationship with celebrities is more complicated than we realise. The strength of our interest in celebrities, say academics, may affect our mood.

8 Lynn McCutcheon, of DeVry University in Florida, John Maltby, of Leicester University, and two colleagues will publish a book next year exposing the psychological needs and drives behind celebrity worship.

9 But initial results of research they have conducted show that about a third of people suffer from what the researchers call "celebrity worship syndrome" and it affects their mental wellbeing.

10 It raises a troubling question: in the era of "industrialised fame", is hero worship bad for you?

11 Perhaps we should blame the start of it on Alexander the Great who, more than 2,000 years ago, exploited to the full the idea of the beautiful "god-king".

12 But if celebrity has been a cultural phenomenon for centuries, why should it have become a problem now? McCutcheon and Maltby believe the scale of it has made a huge jump in recent years. The average westerner is now exposed to hundreds of star images every day, through advertising, broadcasting, fashion, the internet and innumerable other forms.

13 Though sales of some celebrity magazines are slipping, figures show that new publications are thriving. In America, the thirst for star images is so strong that one photographer was recently paid £70,000 for a single picture.

14 David Beckham is now so famous that one paper set out on a humorous quest to find someone who did not know who he was: they finally tracked down an innocent in the Saharan city of Timbuktu.

15 The rapid growth of fan-based internet sites spreads gossip, the lifeblood of celebrity, at lightning speed. There are

more than 100,000 sites dedicated to Madonna alone.

16 Such a speedy development has prompted the academics to create the celebrity attitude scale. Using a series of questions designed to gauge personality and the level of interest in celebrities, they surveyed 700 people.

17 Most were just casually interested in stars. But one in five people displayed a determined interest. They even rearrange their social lives, for example, to follow their chosen celebrity.

18 Some 10% of people displayed such "intense-personal" attitudes towards celebrities that they showed signs of addiction.

19 It can lead to extreme actions. On both sides of the Atlantic, some fans have resorted to plastic surgery to look more like their heroes. A Scottish actor had himself turned into a Pierce Brosnan lookalike and admits he now often walks and talks like 007.

20 Dr Nicholas Chugay, a Beverly Hills surgeon, has turned various Californians into Elvis Presley or Cher. "I have had to turn some people away because I do not feel it would be good for them to let such worship take over their lives," said Chugay.

21 BUT it may not be all that bad. Indeed, other academics argue that the likes of Beckham and Madonna are even good for you. They say that celebrity culture is based on sound reasons: by watching and imitating our so-called betters, whether it be in clothes or habits, we learn to flourish in human society.

22 Francisco Gil-White, of Pennsylvania University, argues we need celebrities to show us the road to success. He says they provide the educational and entertaining fables once sought in fairy tales.

23 "It makes sense to copy winners, because whoever is getting more of what everybody wants, and in this society this includes media attention, is probably using successful methods to get it."

24 But though some role models, such as Gareth Gates, the singer, and Tiger Woods, the golfer, can maintain they are blazing a trail for others to follow, can less worthy idols cause damage? Nancy Salzburg, who is researching charisma at San Diego University, said bad idols can cause trouble for their followers.

25 Choose well and there are benefits in celebrity, says Maltby. "It may help people to develop a relationship with and understand the world. If you admire someone like David Beckham, for example, and follow his dietary regime and the way he plays football, there can be a positive outcome in doing that."

26 Mark Griffiths, a professor of psychology at Nottingham Trent University, agrees.

27 "It was quite clear that for fans their idols formed a healthy part of their life," he said. "It was a way of raising their self-esteem.

28 What has happened is that people are not so religious and they don't look up to political and religious leaders any more. They have been replaced by the David Beckhams and the pop stars and film stars. That's who you see on the walls of teenagers' rooms because these are the people they look up to and admire."

Adapted from an article by
John Harlow

[*END OF PASSAGE*]

[BLANK PAGE]

FOR OFFICIAL USE

G

Total Mark

0860/404

NATIONAL QUALIFICATIONS 2005

WEDNESDAY, 4 MAY
1.00 PM – 1.50 PM

ENGLISH
STANDARD GRADE
General Level
Reading
Questions

Fill in these boxes and read what is printed below.

Full name of centre

Town

Forename(s)

Surname

Date of birth
Day Month Year

Scottish candidate number

Number of seat

NB Before leaving the examination room you must give this booklet to the invigilator. If you do not, you may lose all the marks for this paper.

SCOTTISH QUALIFICATIONS AUTHORITY

Marks

QUESTIONS

Write your answers in the spaces provided.

Look at Paragraphs 1 and 2.

1. What evidence is there to suggest that Katherine Hicks was a keen fan of Boyzone?

Memorobilia She has.

~~Money She has spend ton tickets~~

sor concerts newspaper clipings

2 1 0

2. **Write down three key facts** which clearly show that Katherine Hicks is now a keen Westlife fan. 2 1 0

(i) attension had moved on.

(ii) ~~She [illegible]~~ such a reguler at concerts they recognise her.

(iii) Money spent on tickets.

Look at Paragraph 3.

3. Why do you think the writer uses the expression "fixed her sights"?

This expresses that she has dropped her like for westlife and concentrated on David Sneddon.

2 ■ 0

4. "early days in her "acquaintance" with him"

Why has the writer put the word "acquaintance" in inverted commas?

As he is being sarcastick. (she is not really an acquaintance to any band although she thinks she is)

2 ■ 0

5. What do the words "forced" and "indignantly" in Paragraph 3 tell you about Katherine's reactions to the TV presenter's treatment of David Sneddon?

That she was annoyed at the reporters and wanted to help david badly.

2 1 0

PAGE TOTAL

Marks

Look at Paragraphs 4 to 6.

6. "Hicks is no deluded young teen: she is a 28-year-old electrical engineer." (Paragraph 4)

   What does this statement tell you about the writer's attitude towards Katherine's behaviour?

   That She is to old to bet doing what teenagers do. — 2 ■ 0

7. (*a*) Which of the following best describes Katherine's attitude towards her "addiction"?

   Tick (✓) the appropriate box.

   Concerned ☐

   Guilty ☐

   Relaxed ☑ — 2 ■ 0

   (*b*) **Quote an expression** to support your answer.

   "but it has never caused me Problems" — 2 ■ 0

Look at Paragraphs 7 to 10.

8. **Give three reasons** why psychologists are showing an increasing interest in "celebrity culture". — 2 1 0

   (i) they assert our mood.

   (ii) Assects some mentat wellbeing.

   (iii) As 1/3 of People now suffer from CWS.

9. Explain why the writer ends Paragraph 10 with a question.

   As he wants the reader to give his own oppinion, — 2 ■ 0

PAGE TOTAL

Marks

Look at Paragraphs 11 to 14.

10. Who does the writer suggest is to blame for the start of hero worship?

alexander the great.

2 0

11. **Quote an expression** which shows that celebrity worship is nothing new.

"more than 2,000 years ago"

2 0

12. **In your own words** explain why the scale of hero worship has made a huge jump in recent years.

As their is more publisity on stars now, and peopa see more of them every day.

2 1 0

13. What does the word "thirst" suggest about the American attitude towards celebrity gossip?

That they need it badly, like human's need water.

2 0

14. Why do you think the writer includes the information about the quest in Paragraph 14?

To show that it is only peopa in parts of the world with limited resources t.v.s etc that dont know about David beckham

2 1 0

Look at Paragraphs 15 to 18.

15. What has helped to spread celebrity gossip at great speed?

The rapid growth of fan based internet sites.

2 0

PAGE TOTAL

Marks

16. In your own words what is the "celebrity attitude scale" designed to reveal?

How much the person admired a celebrity

2 1 0

Look at Paragraphs 19 and 20.

17. In what **two** ways does the writer show the extent of celebrity "addiction"? 2 1 0

(i) Plastic surgury to look like their hero

(ii) ~~rearranged their life around the celebritys~~ to follow them. it can lead to extreme actions

Look at Paragraphs 21 to 24.

18. Why does the writer put the word "BUT" in capital letters at the beginning of Paragraph 21?

As he is trying to explain to the reader that liking celebritys it is not all doom and gloom

2 1 0

19. In the opinion of Francisco Gil-White, what important influence have celebrities replaced?

fairy tales

2 ■ 0

20. What does the writer's use of the expression "blazing a trail" (Paragraph 24) tell you about Gareth Gates and Tiger Woods?

It means that they are setting an example.

2 ■ 0

[Turn over for Questions 21, 22 and 23 on *Page six*

PAGE TOTAL

Marks

Look at Paragraphs 25 to 28.

21. **In your own words** what, according to Maltby, could be the positive outcomes of admiring David Beckham?

you can become fitter and healthier if you follow the way david beckham controls his life.

2 1 0

22. According to Mark Griffiths:

(*a*) how can idols form a healthy part of people's lives?

Answer in your own words.

As some People have no religion to look to so they look to positive rolemodels and this can help raise their self esteam

2 ■ 0

(*b*) why have pop stars and film stars replaced political and religious leaders?

Tick (✓) the appropriate box.

They are good looking.	☐
They are easily recognised.	☐
They are respected and highly regarded.	✓

2 ■ 0

Think about the passage as a whole.

23. "DAZZLED BY THE STARS"

Explain why, in your opinion, this is an **appropriate** title.

As stars in the sky are Dazzeling and celebrities are reffered to as stars and are also ~~reffered to~~ described as being dazzling & beutiful

2 1 0

[*END OF QUESTION PAPER*]

PAGE TOTAL

FOR OFFICIAL USE

p2	
p3	
p4	
p5	
p6	
TOTAL MARK	

[BLANK PAGE]

[BLANK PAGE]

[BLANK PAGE]

[BLANK PAGE]

F
G
C

0860/407

NATIONAL QUALIFICATIONS 2003

TUESDAY, 6 MAY
9.00 AM – 10.15 AM

ENGLISH
STANDARD GRADE
Foundation, General and Credit Levels
Writing

Read This First

1 Inside this booklet, there are photographs and words.
Use them to help you when you are thinking about what to write.
Look at all the material and think about all the possibilities.

2 There are 22 assignments altogether for you to choose from.

3 Decide which assignment you are going to attempt.
Choose only **one** and write its number in the margin of your answer book.

4 Pay close attention to what you are asked to write.
Plan what you are going to write.
Read and check your work before you hand it in.
Any changes to your work should be made clearly.

SCOTTISH QUALIFICATIONS AUTHORITY

FIRST **Look at the picture opposite.**
It shows someone walking across a bridge into the fog.

NEXT Think about a place with an eerie, mysterious atmosphere.

WHAT YOU HAVE TO WRITE

1. **Write a story** using the following opening.

   Jan squared her shoulders and steeled herself against the biting cold. Staring ahead intently, she strode off into the chill fog . . .

OR

2. Sometimes in darkest winter, all we want to do is huddle up in front of the fire and . . .

   Write about a special memory of such an occasion.

   You should include your **thoughts and feelings.**

OR

3. **Write in any way you choose** using the picture opposite as your inspiration.

OR

4. **Write a short story** using **ONE** of the following titles:

   The Stranger   The Fog   Into the Darkness

[Turn over

FIRST **Look at the picture opposite.**
It shows a spider's web.

NEXT Think about feeling trapped or being in danger.

WHAT YOU HAVE TO WRITE

5. **Write about an incident** in your life when you felt that there was no escape.

   Remember to include your **thoughts and feelings.**

OR

6. **Write in any way you choose** using **ONE** of the following titles:

   The Web Trapped The Net

OR

7. The natural world is in danger if we do not take steps to protect it.

   Write your views.

[Turn over

FIRST **Look at the picture opposite.**
It shows a picture of a fantasy hero.

NEXT Think about action heroes/heroines.

WHAT YOU HAVE TO WRITE

8. Fantasy heroes/heroines make good role models for the young.

Write your views.

OR

9. Write about a time when you felt that your actions were heroic.

Remember to include your **thoughts and feelings.**

OR

10. Violence on the screen encourages violence in real life.

Discuss.

OR

11. **Write a short story** using the title:

The Warrior.

[Turn over

CCTV
in
operation

FIRST **Look at the picture opposite.**
It shows a CCTV camera sign.

NEXT Think about your privacy.

WHAT YOU HAVE TO WRITE

12. CCTV cameras and curfews are effective but unpopular methods of cutting crime.

Discuss.

OR

13. Write about an occasion in your life when you were caught doing something wrong.

Remember to include your **thoughts and feelings.**

OR

14. Write a short story using the following title:

Caught on Camera.

[Turn over

FIRST **Look at the picture opposite.**
It shows a wave crashing against a sea wall.

NEXT Think about the power of nature.

WHAT YOU HAVE TO WRITE

15. Write about a time when you were caught in bad weather.

You should include your **thoughts and feelings.**

OR

16. Winters get windier; summers get wetter.

Write about your views on our changing climate.

OR

17. **Write a short story** using **ONE** of the following titles:

The Storm The Force

OR

18. Storm Damage Widespread.

Write a newspaper report using this headline.

[Turn over for assignments 19 to 22 on *Page twelve*

There are no pictures for these assignments.

Describe the scene brought to mind by **ONE** of the following:

19. "A ship is floating in the harbour now,
A wind is hovering o'er the mountain's brow . . ."

P B Shelley

OR

"The woods are lovely, dark and deep . . ."

Robert Frost

OR

"All shod with steel
We hissed along the polished ice . . ."

William Wordsworth

OR

20. My Ideal Webpage.

What features would you include in your ideal webpage and why?

OR

21. Today we have too many rights and not enough responsibilities.

Do you agree or disagree?

Write your views.

OR

22. **Write a short story** entitled:

The Attic.

[*END OF QUESTION PAPER*]

[BLANK PAGE]

[BLANK PAGE]

[BLANK PAGE]

F
G
C

0860/407

NATIONAL
QUALIFICATIONS
2004

WEDNESDAY, 5 MAY
9.00 AM – 10.15 AM

ENGLISH
STANDARD GRADE
Foundation, General
and Credit Levels
Writing

Read This First

1 Inside this booklet, there are photographs and words.
Use them to help you when you are thinking about what to write.
Look at all the material and think about all the possibilities.

2 There are 22 assignments altogether for you to choose from.

3 Decide which assignment you are going to attempt.
Choose only **one** and write its number in the margin of your answer book.

4 Pay close attention to what you are asked to write.
Plan what you are going to write.
Read and check your work before you hand it in.
Any changes to your work should be made clearly.

SCOTTISH
QUALIFICATIONS
AUTHORITY

FIRST **Look at the picture opposite.**
It shows a picture of a communications satellite.

NEXT Think about the advantages and disadvantages of communications technology.

WHAT YOU HAVE TO WRITE

1. The more television channels there are, the harder it is to find something good to watch.

Do you agree or disagree?

Give your views.

OR

2. **Write a short story** in which a mobile phone plays an important part.

OR

3. The Internet continues to make the world smaller.

Write about the **advantages and disadvantages** of the Internet.

[Turn over

[0860/407] *Page four*

FIRST **Look at the pictures opposite.**
They show a young woman staring over mountain peaks, and a city scene.

NEXT Think about special places you have visited.

WHAT YOU HAVE TO WRITE

4. **Write about** whether you would prefer to live in the city or the country.

   Give reasons for your choice.

   OR

5. **Write in any way you choose** using **one or both** of the pictures as your inspiration.

   OR

6. A view I will always remember.

   Write about a place which had this effect on you.

   OR

7. **Write a short story** with the title:

   No Time to Spare

[Turn over

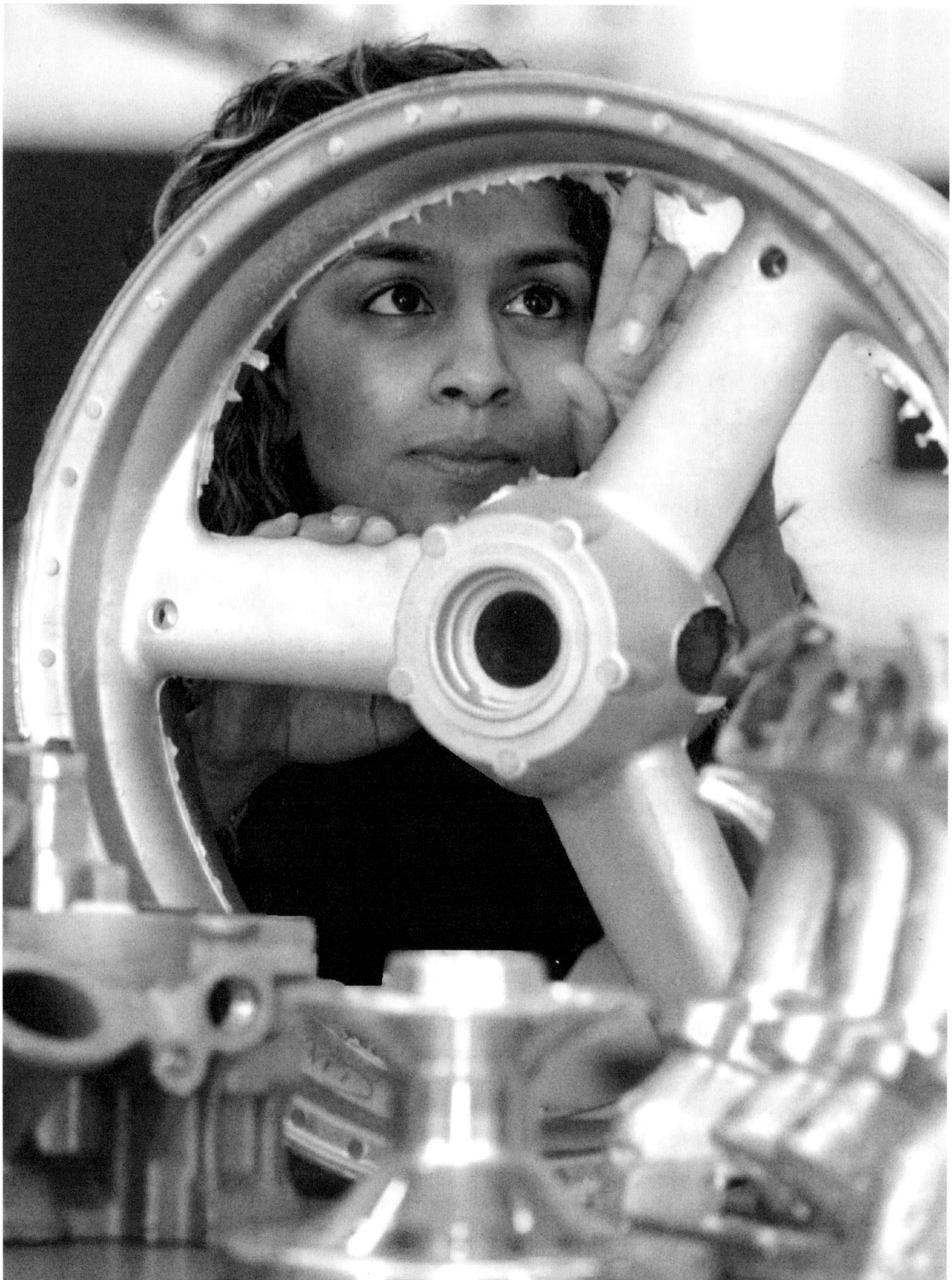

FIRST **Look at the picture opposite.**
It shows a student looking through the hub of a wheel.

NEXT Think about the world of work.

WHAT YOU HAVE TO WRITE

8. **Write an informative article** for your school magazine on a career which you want to follow when you leave school.

OR

9. In our everyday lives we depend too much on machines.

Discuss.

OR

10. **Write a letter** to a local newspaper putting the case for more education for work.

OR

11. **Write about** an occasion in your life when teamwork was vital.

Remember to include your **thoughts and feelings.**

[Turn over

FIRST **Look at the picture opposite.**
It shows a young boy winning a race.

NEXT Think about what it feels like to take part in an event.

WHAT YOU HAVE TO WRITE

12. **Write about** an achievement you remember above all others.

    Remember to include your **thoughts and feelings.**

    OR

13. Communities today do not have enough organised events to suit young people.

    Discuss.

    OR

14. "It is the taking part that is important, not the winning."

    Do you agree or disagree?

    Give your views.

    OR

15. **Write a short story** using the title:

    Crossing The Line

[Turn over

FIRST **Look at the picture opposite.**
It shows a man looking out of his house window over a city.

NEXT Think about what it feels like to be different.

WHAT YOU HAVE TO WRITE

16. **Write a short story** about a character who is isolated from society.

OR

17. **Write in any way you choose** using **one** of the following titles:

Keeper of the City Success The Glass House

OR

18. **Write a description** of your ideal home.

OR

19. Even famous people have a right to privacy.

Do you agree or disagree?

Give your views.

[Turn over for assignments 20 to 22 on *Page twelve*

There are no pictures for these assignments.

20. "Shop till you drop."

Retail therapy does more harm than good.

Discuss.

OR

21. Describe the scene brought to mind by **one** of the following:

For winter rains and ruins are over,
And all the season of snows

Swinburne

OR

He will watch from dawn to gloom
The lake-reflected sun

Shelley

OR

The rocky summits, split and rent,
Formed turret, dome, or battlement

Scott

22. Write a short story using the title:

Appearances Can Be Deceptive

[*END OF QUESTION PAPER*]

[BLANK PAGE]

F
G
C

0860/407

NATIONAL QUALIFICATIONS 2005

WEDNESDAY, 4 MAY
9.00 AM – 10.15 AM

ENGLISH
STANDARD GRADE
Foundation, General and Credit Levels
Writing

Read This First

1 Inside this booklet, there are photographs and words.
Use them to help you when you are thinking about what to write.
Look at all the material and think about all the possibilities.

2 There are 23 assignments altogether for you to choose from.

3 Decide which assignment you are going to attempt.
Choose only **one** and write its number in the margin of your answer book.

4 Pay close attention to what you are asked to write.
Plan what you are going to write.
Read and check your work before you hand it in.
Any changes to your work should be made clearly.

SCOTTISH QUALIFICATIONS AUTHORITY

SAB 0860/407 6/70570

STOP

FIRST **Look at the picture opposite.**
It shows a holiday scene.

NEXT Think about holidays.

WHAT YOU HAVE TO WRITE

1. Even the worst holiday can have its funny side.

Write about your experience of a holiday like this.

Remember to include your **thoughts and feelings**.

OR

2. **Write an article for a magazine describing** your favourite holiday resort and outlining its main attractions.

OR

3. Sun, sea and sand.

Surely there must be more to a holiday than that?

Do you agree or disagree? Give your views.

OR

4. **Write a short story** entitled:

Going Places.

[Turn over

FIRST **Look at the picture opposite.**
It shows a train in a station at night.

NEXT Think about journeys by train.

WHAT YOU HAVE TO WRITE

5. **Write about** a memorable train journey.
Remember to include your **thoughts and feelings.**

OR

6. Trains and railways are fascinating but can be dangerous.
Discuss.

OR

7. **Write a short story** using **ONE** of the following titles:
Night Train The Deserted Station Crossing The Border

OR

8. Trainspotting—an unusual hobby?
Do you have a hobby which some people might consider unusual?
Write about it, making it clear why **you** enjoy it.

[Turn over

FIRST **Look at the picture opposite.**
It shows a father coaching his son.

NEXT Think about competitive sport.

WHAT YOU HAVE TO WRITE

9. Young people today are under too much pressure to succeed.

Do you agree or disagree? Give your views.

OR

10. **Write about** an occasion when you took part in a sporting activity and lost.

Remember to include your **thoughts and feelings.**

OR

11. **Write a short story** entitled:

Determination.

OR

12. Playing in a team has much more to offer than competing as an individual.

Do you agree or disagree? Give your views.

[Turn over

FIRST **Look at the picture opposite.**
It shows an iceberg.

NEXT Think about the beauty and danger of icebergs.

WHAT YOU HAVE TO WRITE

13. **Write in any way you choose** using the picture opposite as your inspiration.

OR

14. **Write a newspaper article** using the headline:

Ship Strikes Iceberg!

OR

15. Global warming will end us if we do not end it.

Do you agree or disagree? Give your views.

OR

16. **Write a short story** using **ONE** of the following titles:

Iceworld Hidden Depths

[Turn over

FIRST **Look at the pictures opposite.**
They show amateur and professional performers.

NEXT Think about live performance.

WHAT YOU HAVE TO WRITE

17. Write about an occasion when you
either took part in a live performance
or helped behind the scenes.
Remember to include your **thoughts and feelings.**

OR

18. Television shows such as *Pop Idol* do more harm than good.
Discuss.

OR

19. Write a short story using **ONE** of the following titles:
The Fame Game Practice Makes Perfect

[Turn over for assignments 20 to 23 on *Page twelve*

There are no pictures for these assignments.

20. Write a letter using the following opening.

Dear Sir/Madam,

I am writing to complain in the strongest possible terms about . . .

OR

21. Describe the scene brought to mind by the following:

"Scarring the very sky, they scrape and scratch ever upwards, those rectangles of glass and stone—our so modern office blocks."

OR

22. Letter-writing today is not dead; it has simply been updated by e-mail, texting and messaging.

Discuss.

OR

23. Write a short story using **ONE** of the following openings.

Make sure that you develop **character** and **setting** as well as **plot**.

A cruel smile played on Kane's lips as he swung open the heavy door and stepped out into the cold, grim world . . .

OR

It was a misty morning in late November and Jane was late. Frantically late. She quickened her step . . .

OR

Tom was puzzled. Well, perhaps more perplexed than puzzled. He sat staring, wide-eyed, at the letter on the table . . .

[*END OF QUESTION PAPER*]

[BLANK PAGE]

[BLANK PAGE]

[BLANK PAGE]

Acknowledgements

Leckie & Leckie is grateful to the copyright holders, as credited, for permission to use their material:
The Scotsman for the article 'The House Bunny Bug' by Gillian Ferguson and the accompanying photograph by Ian Rutherford (2002 Foundation Reading paper p 2);
'We're out for the Count' by Catriona Marchant © *The Times*, London, 13 October 2001 (2003 General Reading paper p 2);
Allstar Picture Library for a photograph (2003 Writing paper p 6);
Faber & Faber for an extract from 'Ghostly Hauntings' by Ted Hughes (2004 Foundation Reading paper p 2–3);
The Mail on Sunday for the article 'Pucker way to kiss a hummingbird' by Mark Carwardine (2004 General Reading paper p 2);
The BBC for a photograph (2004 General Reading paper p 2);
Getty Images for a photograph (2004 Writing paper p 2);
Getty Images for a photograph (2004 Writing paper p 8);
Camera Press, London, for a photograph by John Swannell (2004 Writing paper p 10);
The Sunday Times for the article 'Dazzling the Stars' by John Harlow (2005 General Reading paper p 2);
FreeFoto.com for a photograph (2005 Writing paper p 4);
The Scotsman for a photograph (2005 Writing paper p 6);
Ralph A. Clevenger/Corbis for a photograph (2005 Writing paper p 8).

The following companies/individuals have very generously given permission to reproduce their copyright material free of charge:
Catherine Czerkawska for an article from *The Scotsman* (2001 General Reading paper p 2);
Michael Munro for an extract from *Application* (2002 General Reading paper pp 2–3);
FreeFoto.com for 4 photographs (2003 Writing paper pp 2, 4, 8 &10);
Maurice Lacroix Ltd for an advertisement (2004 Writing paper p 4);
Newsquest Media Group for a photograph (2004 Writing paper p 4);
News Team International for a photograph (2004 Writing paper p 6);
The House of Lochar Publishers for an extract from *Think Me Back* by Catherine Forde (2005 Foundation Reading paper pp 2–4);
Newsquest Media Group for a photograph (2005 Writing paper p 10);
TES Scotland for a photograph (2005 Writing paper p 10).